Praise for

God forgive us for thinking too high~~...~~ ~~...~~ ~~...~~ thinking too lowly of ourselves. God forgive us for thinking of ourselves so much... Mark Sayers offers a brilliant corrective here to a society that is self absorbed, narcissistic and aching for transcendence. You can hear the whisper that you are beloved . . . and you can hear the persistent call that if we really want to find our lives, then we need to give our lives away for others.

SHANE CLAIBORNE, author, activist, and recovering sinner

http://www.thesimpleway.org

Every age has a unique way of distorting our sense of self, and we often only recognize our mistakes in hindsight. Many are able to identify the pitfalls of modern individualism, but Sayers insightfully examines our self obsession in a timely manner and offers a biblical path to transformation. I love this book!

CHRIS SEAY, pastor of Ecclesia Houston and
author of *The Gospel According to Lost*

This timely and insightful book, *The Vertical Self* by Mark Sayers, is exceptional. Well written, remarkably wise, and brimming with sound spiritual discernment, the book is a must-read if we are going to find a way out of the confusing maze of cultural icons and ideologies that are detrimental to our faith and life in Christ. Sayers' assessment and critique of these purveyors of a false self is perceptive and fully on target, while his call and challenge to cultivate a true self is deeply grounded in the reality of God and scripture. Revolutionary Christian thinking, so necessary in an age like ours, is a trademark of Sayers; and *The Vertical Self* is not merely relevant, but highly urgent.

In my experience of over twenty years of teaching, advising, and wrestling through tough issues with thousands of people at Swiss L'Abri, it has become exceedingly evident to me that loads of them struggle with a devastating attachment to a cultural idolatry, all too often, and most unfortunately, powerfully mirrored inside churches. I believe that Sayers' compelling book will have an enormous impact in helping many turn away from this deathly deception, as it points us to the living God and to the need to embrace the ways of life and truth that only the gospel can provide. Take, read, and apply *The Vertical Self*.

DR. GREGORY J. LAUGHERY, author of several books including *Living Spiritual Rhythms For Today*, and director of L'Abri Fellowship, Switzerland

Cool, as defined by postmodern culture, is an unstable and artificial construct, which is defined only *horizontally* by ephemeral and mercurial cultural vanities. Mark Sayers has a better idea, a biblical idea: the self should be defined and lived out *vertically* before the ultimate reality of God himself. This culturally informed, well-written, biblically rich, and practically helpful book makes holiness both imperative and attractive.

DOUGLAS GROOTHUIS, PHD, professor of philosophy at Denver Seminary

Are we tethered to the shifting sands of the messages of world around us or to the plumb line of God's grace and love? This is the insightful question *The Vertical Self* lays before us. Mark Sayers provides queues and clues of the challenges of communicating God's message of love and grace within contemporary culture whose sense of value is often derived from images and ideas as fleeting as they are unrealistic—a guide for personal examination and mission.

THE REV. CANON ELLIS E. BRUST, Churches for the Sake of Others

Mark is just one of those people who is creatively gifted with a sense of what is important for his generation. In The Vertical Self he probes at the roots of personal transformation—our sense of identity— and he does it with rare cultural savvy combined with genuine theological insight. A unique read.

ALAN HIRSCH, www.theforgottenways.com,
author of The Forgotten Ways and coauthor of Untamed

Reading The Vertical Self, I was convinced that Mark Sayers has correctly identified the malaise that inhabits the western church—a malaise that cannot be addressed by anything other than individual reengagement with God on the deepest level. His sociological insights into the worldviews of the majority of Western Christians were so accurate and incisive I could not think of one church leader who would not benefit from reading this book. This is the most helpful book I have read in the last year and one of the most important I have read in the last decade.

DR. CHERYL CATFORD
National Director, Australian Evangelical Alliance

THE VERTICAL SELF

THE VERTICAL SELF

MARK SAYERS

THOMAS NELSON
Since 1798

NASHVILLE   DALLAS   MEXICO CITY   RIO DE JANEIRO

Published in Nashville, Tennessee, by Thomas Nelson. Thomas Nelson is a registered trademark of Thomas Nelson, Inc.

Thomas Nelson, Inc., titles may be purchased in bulk for educational, business, fund-raising, or sales promotional use. For information, please e-mail SpecialMarkets@thomasnelson.com.

Unless otherwise noted, Scripture quotations are taken from the *Holy Bible, Today's New International Version*®. © 2002, 2004 by International Bible Society. Used by permission of Zondervan Publishing House. All rights reserved.

Library of Congress Cataloging-in-Publication Data

Sayers, Mark.
    The vertical self / Mark Sayers.
        p. cm.
    ISBN 978-0-8499-2000-4 (pbk.)
    1. Identity (Psychology)—Religious aspects—Christianity. 2. Self.
3. Spirituality. 4. Holiness—Christianity. I. Title.
    BV4509.5.S29 2009
    248.4—dc22   2009041497

Printed in the United States of America

10 11 12 13 RRD 6 5 4 3 2 1

For Trudi, who believed in me from the beginning.

Contents

Acknowledgments

Thanks to Matt Baugher for encouraging and believing in me as a writer; thanks to Jenn McNeil for being such a great and understanding editor; thanks also to Rod Schumacher, Brittany Lassiter, Stephanie Newton, Emily Sweeny, and the rest of the fantastic team at Thomas Nelson. Thanks to Matt Deutscher for his work on the visual elements of this book. A big thanks to Len Sweet for his contribution to this book. Thanks also to Trudi, Garry, Joy, and Glen Sayers; Sarah Deutscher; Alan Hirsch; and Raquel Jensen for reading through the first draft and offering feedback. And last but not least, thanks to the Whitehorse-Manningham Regional Library Corporation for saving me a small fortune in books and for a lifetime of learning.

The Divining Rod

> Take away the paradox from a thinker,
> and you have a professor.
>
> —SOREN KIERKEGAARD

ieter Bruegel is my favorite Renaissance painter. Of his fifty
or so surviving works, my two front-runners are *The Tower
of Babel* (1563) and *The Fight Between Carnival and Lent*
(1559). The stunning feature of *The Tower of Babel* is how much it
looks like a Roman coliseum, a structure warily familiar to the early
Christians. The stunning feature of *The Fight Between Carnival
and Lent* is its mocking mash-up of the two contradictory seasons
of the Christian calendar, as symbolized in the jousting match in
the foreground. A bustling town square is filled with jarring jux-
tapositions of fat merrymakers, musicians, dancers, and jesters
competing for visual attention with bony almsgivers—purposeful,
prudish, and scholarly in their fasting and sobriety.[1]

One uniqueness of Christianity is its ability to bring opposites
together without reconciling them in some synthesis or extrud-
ing them by some mean middle. For fifteen hundred years both
Carnival and Lent, two opposing but complementary aspects of

Christian faith, came to be celebrated in their fullness as part of a very complex liturgical calendar that structured people's lives around these polar seasons. In one there was abstinence, sacrifice, sorrow, and "this is a good day to die" mortifications. In the other there was enjoyment, consumption, joy, and "this is a good day to live" celebrations. As historian Eamon Duffy likes to put it, "To fifteenth- and early sixteenth-century sensibilities, the liturgical year was spread over twelve months, not six, and *none of it was secular*."[2] But all of its sacredness was built around opposites fertilizing each other.

With the Protestant Reformation, Lent beat Carnival to a pulp. Feasting as a ritual celebration was deemed gluttonous, The Lord's Supper became a metaphor, and wakes and weddings became more reveries than revelries. Festive eating and carnivalesque festivities may have continued in folk culture, but the "official" religious culture not only didn't bring the ends together but denied there was more than one end. The Christian art of extremity took the form less of the coincidence of opposites than the collision of opposites.

Few Christian thinkers have understood the nondualist character of Christianity better than G. K. Chesterton, who almost couldn't write a sentence without saying two opposite things at the same time: "Courage . . . means a strong desire to live taking the form of a readiness to die."[3] In fact, Chesterton gave us perhaps the best metaphor for paradox in history: "Truth standing on its head with both legs dangling to gain attention."[4]

Mark Sayers accomplishes such a feat in *The Vertical Self*. In one sense, this book is part of a long history of inquiry into the self. Probably the first in-depth account of the self is in Plato's *Republic*, written around 370 BC. But as Sayers shows in this book, the kind of "self" we know today has a very brief history. For example, the phrase *self-fulfillment* is a nineteenth-century one, with no precedence in history until then. Most Christian "bestsellers" today, little more than self-centeredness wrapped in spirituality, would have been incomprehensible to our ancestors. And what Sayers calls the "horizontal self," or self-differentiated living, has become so dominant that we need the return of the "vertical self," or God-differentiated living. Transcendence is found in de-selfing the self through self-emptying and self-giving

Or to put it in the language of paradox, the cruciform life requires the "crossing" of the horizontal and the vertical. In fact, Christian heresy is the cross uncrossed. Christian truth is built on paradox, on bringing the vertical and the horizontal together. In fact, orthodoxy is paradoxy.[5] Christianity asks you to be who you are and who you aren't at the same time. The paradox of Christian faith, its ability simultaneously to possess and dispossess its possessor, its imperishability depending on its inconstancy, is reflected in the paradox of Christ's life-in-death at work in us: "We are always carrying in the body the death of Jesus, so that the life of Jesus may also be made visible in our bodies" (2 Cor. 4:10).

Living in paradox is like using a divining rod . . . You hold on to the fork-shaped branch for dear life as you let go of your control and let it guide you. Suddenly you find the vibrations veering you in directions where you find things you never expected. That is what this book did for me, as it steered me to streams of living water deep inside my soul that I never knew existed.

—Leonard Sweet

We Need to Change the Conversation

C hristian leaders are engaged in a conversation about what kind of church shape will be most effective in the soil of twenty-first-century Western culture. Books, blogs, and conferences are the arenas in which this discussion is played out. All kinds of answers have been proposed and put into practice. We are told that the church must be more missional, more contemporary, more media savvy, more emerging, more social-justice focused, more seeker sensitive, more liturgical. We have been told that the church of the future will be multisite, small and organic, simple, large, conservative, liberal, postmodern, ancient-future, Celtic, cellular, neomonastic, and incarnational.

Now, I don't want to mock these valid explorations; I come as someone who, for the last seventeen years, has been involved full time in innovative church planting and missions in the highly secular soil of Melbourne, Australia. I have lectured, consulted, and taught on the kinds of churches that I think will reach Western culture. About four years ago, however, a creeping doubt began to enter my mind:

All our attempts to reshape Church in the West will at best be sabotaged and at worst fail because there is a huge unnamed problem with people inside the Church.

As I traveled around speaking at churches of all shapes, approaches, and flavors, I noticed that despite their completely different approaches, they had a common problem. It did not matter if the church was a small, emerging missional community; a traditional liturgical church on the corner; or a multisite contemporary megachurch. There was a basic problem of discipleship. The best way to describe the problem was to say that it was a crisis of identity.

IDENTITY CRISIS

I discovered that the missional strategy taken by churches was neutered because the people inside churches were suffering from an identity crisis. They seemed filled with insecurity about who they were and what difference their faith made in their lives. Jesus' mandate to go out and preach the gospel in Mark 16:15 seemed to have been replaced by the maxim to "go into the world and convince people that you are not a Christian dork."

I would preach at megachurches in the suburbs, led by wonderful leaders whose hearts burned to see their community come to know Christ, yet who would tell me that they often worried that the baby boomers in their congregation were more concerned about what the brand of the SUV they drove said about them than about sharing Christ with their neighbors. I would spend time in the inner city with young mission leaders who had planted incarnational communities in the hardest of soil. They were leaders whose eyes would well up with tears as they shared about their desire to see the poor served and the post-Christian young adults in their community reached, yet who would also be driven to frustration by the fact that their communities were overrun by Christian hipsters more concerned with developing their cool credentials and deconstructing their faith than engaging in genuine mission. I would speak at youth events where youth pastors would sit and pour out their hearts to me, telling me of Christian teens who had taken their own lives because they felt ugly and unattractive; of the epidemic of eating disorders in youth groups; of Christian teen girls sending images of themselves naked to boys' cell phones in order to impress them; of the almost unbearable pressure on teens to be cool, sexy, or famous in order to feel worthwhile as human beings. I even saw this pressure creeping into the lives of leaders, as they felt the demands of dressing cool; of seeming young, fresh, and hip; of managing their personal "brand" online; of making it into the stratosphere of Christian celebrity leaders. I have seen leaders unconsciously starting to confuse their calling with self-promotion as they were lured into the cult of cool.

I began to realize that our lives have stopped speaking to the culture around us. The world looks at us and we look almost exactly the same as the world. Slowly, inch by inch, we have replaced the biblical command to be holy with the quest for status. One of the reasons the early church grew at such a phenomenal rate was that the lives of the early Christians spoke so strongly to their neighbors. There was something different about them, something that spoke of another reality, an alternative way of living, to the culture around them. The early Christians lived lives of holiness that drew others to them and their life-giving message. The early church understood that their identity was rooted in Christ, not the surrounding culture. Therefore it is no wonder that across the Western world so few are coming to know Christ, while thousands exit the church back door.

Yes, we need to discuss how we can shape the church, but we

must also discuss how we have been shaped by our culture. To fail to do so will mean that all our endeavors will come to naught.

I believe that we need a revolution in how we think about church.

But I believe, perhaps more importantly, that we need a revolution of the self.

Introduction

I will also give each of them a white stone with a new name
written on it, known only to the one who receives it.

—REVELATION 2:17

A sexy nurse and a gothic porcelain doll were chained together in a Tokyo street. You see some strange things as you walk around Tokyo's youth-culture district of Harajuku, but this took the cake. No one else seemed to notice, but I was stopped in my tracks. Two girls cut through the crowd of teenage shoppers. To be noticed among the millions who walk Japan's crowded sidewalks takes some doing. One of the girls was dressed like a nineteenth-century porcelain doll that had found its way into a horror movie: her outfit was immaculate; she had obviously spent hours cultivating her gothic-doll chic. The other girl had a completely different look: high heels, fishnet stockings, and what can only be accurately described as a raunchy nurse's outfit. If that were not weird enough, the girls (who couldn't be more than eighteen years old) were chained together. Yes, you read right—a big honking chain joined them at the wrist. As I stood and stared, I realized this was a carefully scripted performance. I looked around for cameras to see if this was one of those crazy Japanese reality-TV shows. But these girls did not need a TV audience; their audience was the people around them. Here I was in the Japan of the Shinto religion and Zen Buddhism, and yet Japanese young people were looking to an altogether different tradition in order to express their identities and find meaning. They were simply playing the game that millions of young adults do around the world. Because we are now unsure of our identities, we play the game of creating and acting out identities.

No longer does our culture provide us with a foundation upon which to build an identity. We have lost the art of forging character, and thus we find ourselves adrift, lost in a sea of insecurity—we do not know who we are. We have given up on finding our true selves, so instead of being ourselves, we act. We no longer work on nurturing our souls; we now construct an image. The girls I saw in Japan were acting in a performance that is repeated all over the world. The details may be different, but the themes are the same: we no longer understand our true selves, so we act.

SEARCHING FOR OUR REAL NAMES

The British reality show *The Monastery* featured a group of secular men, nonbelievers, who for several weeks lived as monks in a Roman Catholic monastery. They attended worship, joined in the prayers, received spiritual direction, and spent time in silence, meditation, and ancient Christian ritual. The show is a fascinating exploration of how secular people integrate a deeply religious experience into their lives and worldviews. In the last episode, it became time for the group to leave the monastery. One of the group, a young man who worked in the porn industry, had his final session of spiritual direction with one of the monks. He came to the conclusion (almost to his own disbelief) that he did not want to return to his ordinary life. The camera captured this discussion as it happened. The young man, with obvious difficulty, shared with the monk that he did not want to return home. He was struggling to find the language to describe what was happening to him. He shared that his fear was that when he returned home, he would lose what he had learned at the monastery. There were a few moments of silence before the monk began to speak. Slowly and gently he told the young man that he had a name, but he also had a name that he did not know. He described how in the book of Revelation we are told that our true names are written in heaven on white stones, that this name on the stone is our real name, pointing to our real identity, who we really are.

As the monk was speaking, the young man's body language showed he was extremely uncomfortable. Remember: this is a secular, British working-class bloke who was involved in the production of porn. This is not someone who was comfortable talking about his feelings or sharing in a profound spiritual discussion. The monk told the young man that he would like to give him a present to take with him as he left the monastery. He reached into his pocket; pulled out a smooth, white stone; and handed it to the young man, telling him that this stone represents his true name. It is a symbol of his quest to find out who he really is before God.

At this point it became obvious to the viewing audience that the young man was fighting with every fiber of his being to avoid breaking down into a blubbering mess. His spiritual director, sensitive to his emotional discomfort, asked the young man if he wanted to end the session. He replied yes; however, he didn't move but simply sat there in silence. The monk told him to sit in the moment, that he didn't have to say anything, that what he was experiencing was a spiritual moment, a mystery to be experienced rather than explained. Laying hands on the young man's head, the monk prayed a moving and beautiful prayer of blessing, and the session ended. Back in his room, the young man struggled to find the language to explain to the camera what had just happened to him. He woke up not believing, but now he believes. The young man left his job, began to attend church, and began to meet regularly with his spiritual director.

As I watched, I felt myself deeply moved. It is easy to feel discouraged today as a believer in our secular culture, to buy the line that no one really cares about the spiritual anymore. Yet I realized that deep down, each one of us, Christian or not, is searching for that name on the white rock in the book of Revelation. We are all like the young man in the monastery. We all crave to find our true identities. Each one of us, at a profoundly deep level, no matter what we believe, is being drawn, cajoled, and beckoned by God to our true selves, to find ourselves as God sees us: redeemed and perfect. Yet at the same time, this desire in us is derailed and sabotaged by our culture, which offers imitations of our true identities—faux identities, pseudoselves, and images instead of the image of God. This book is about the quest to find our true selves. It is rooted in the belief that in God's future we exist totally redeemed, exactly as he wants us to be.

However, to find our true selves, to see ourselves as God sees us, we must embark on a journey—a journey of rediscovering holiness, of cultivating our true selves. We must examine the way we have traded our quest for our true selves for the pseudo selves that our culture offers us. And finally, we must come to understand the perfect state of wholeness and peace that God desires for us, and how this peace and balance will lead us to our true selves.

Are you ready to find out who you really are?

CHAPTER 1

Modern Identity

PICK YOUR PERSONALITY

In front of me I have a catalog for cell phones. The front cover of the catalog does not feature a phone or any image at all. There is nothing to show that this catalog is even selling phones. All there is on the cover is one simple word that sums up our age: *me*.

As I open the catalog, I discover that each page extols the virtues of the latest models of phones for the coming season. Each page features a model or models who in some way attempt to match the "personality" of the phone. The first personality I encounter is the image of a beautiful young woman lounging on a piece of rustic outdoor furniture. Behind her is a lake, complete with untouched forest in the distance. Her hair is long and parted down the middle. She is wearing a pair of bell-bottoms; she could have been transported from Woodstock, although she looks slightly more groomed and tanned. The copy at the bottom of the page uses words such as *relaxed* and *spacious living*. I move

1

on from this twenty-first-century hippie with her eco-chic style and bohemian peace and turn the page.

The next ad is in black and white, this one featuring a ruggedly handsome man probably in his early thirties. He wears a large vintage belt buckle and leans on a dirty-looking SUV. He is unshaven, and his clothes look as though they have been lived in. His thumbs are plunged into his pockets—a sign that body-language experts tell us represents sexual aggression—and he is gazing wistfully off into the distance. With his worn jeans and dirty white T-shirt, he could be James Dean's grandson. He is giving off social signals that, when communicated together, are labeled "cool" in our culture.

Another page, another personality. This time it's two young girls on a dance floor. One has a cheeky or naughty expression on her face. The story accompanying the picture tells us that this particular new phone, with its Internet capabilities, is a great way to juggle multiple boyfriends at the same time. The copy features modern-day mantras such as "right now," "sort it out on the fly," "life is random," and the obligatory "social life." The girls look like international models, but one of them, as she looks at the mobile phone, inexplicably seems to be in the midst of sexual ecstasy. The suggestive body language, the clothes, the way one girl looks into the camera seductively, the way the other looks as if she can only be turned on by a cell phone—these all speak of another ubiquitous contemporary personality, the personality of "sexy." I leave behind the pleasure-loving party girls and turn the page.

The picture and feel are different yet again. A young woman stands in the middle of what looks like a Hollywood cocktail party, a city skyline twinkling in the background. She wears a dress that would fit in on the red carpet at the Oscars. She looks like Grace Kelly. In contrast to the people around her, she lights up. Behind her, a stylish and beautiful woman shoots her a glance of envy. She is the epitome of the mysterious quality we label *glamorous*. The ad copy features terms such as *fabulous, daring, stand out,* and *demand attention.*

I turn the page and this time look upon another handsome man, this one in his early forties. He is wearing a suit and sits back confidently at his desk, which overlooks a cityscape. He has the look of power on his face. The text accompanying the picture uses the terms *control, command situations, grab opportunities, powerful,* and *anything is possible.*

Welcome to the twenty-first century, where we can now purchase and change personalities the way we can clothes, depending on mood or circumstance. Welcome to the world in which we are told we can be anyone we want to be, where identity is no longer based in a sense of self but rather in the imagery we choose at any particular moment.

Try this experiment. In three to four sentences, describe what makes someone (a) cool, (b) sexy, (c) glamorous.

How did you do? It's a lot harder than you think, yet many people around the globe use these words to create identities for themselves. How many people use these media-created masks to give off the sense that they have captured these esoteric qualities? Think how many millions, if not trillions of dollars are spent each year on products, clothes, experiences, even property so that people can convince themselves and others that these adjectives describe them and that they are, therefore, valuable members of our society. Cool, sexy, glamorous: these are the new social virtues.

Social virtues existed in the past. Society in the Middle Ages valued chivalry and saintliness. The culture of the early modern period upheld the concept of gentlemanliness. Jewish culture celebrated the *mensch*—a fair and good person. Social virtues have existed in almost every culture on earth, but now our social virtues have become these disposable masks: cool, sexy, bohe-mian, cosmopolitan, tough . . . the list goes on. We have gotten to this point because we have lost a sense of self. All we can do now is act; we deal in superficial imagery rather than in our God-given image. We have lost our identities and don't know how to get them back.

HOW DID WE BEGIN TO LOSE OUR IDENTITIES?

Peter went backpacking in Thailand to find himself. Patricia's new relationship has made her feel centered. Since Dave got that new job, he seems grounded. What do these statements really mean? Had Peter lost himself the way one loses his keys? What was Patricia when she was single—de-centered? What on earth was going on with Dave? Was he stuck in lunar orbit before he became grounded? The ways we describe ourselves today are indications that we have become unstuck; we have lost our sense of ourselves. We are at a unique time in history. Our world has gone through intense political, economic, social, and technologi-cal change. But we often forget that at a personal level we have gone through intense changes in the way we process identity. Our understanding of self and the way we construct a sense of identity are unprecedented in human history.

In the year 1863, my great-great-grandfather Hermann Carl Franz Huth emigrated to Australia from the province of Prussia in what is today eastern Germany. My mother recently found some photos of him and my great-grandmother looking ancient with many of my other German forebears. In the photo they are having a picnic in the Aussie bush. Now, the area in which this picnic is taking place is quite hot even in winter, yet there they are in their immaculate outfits—suits, waistcoats, and so on. Today if we were going to have a picnic in such a place, the choice of attire would be shorts, tank tops, T-shirts, flip-flops, and plenty of sunscreen. Even in shorts we would probably be dripping with sweat, yet here are these people from a different time with their different values and clothing and mannerisms. Even the way they sit and lounge seems more formal, and the children seem more adult. Theirs was a completely different way of looking at life and the world; it was a different way of relating to and interacting with the culture around them. Such formality is almost unknown to us today; back then formality and convention were keys to developing an identity. We've changed a lot since then.

If you lived one hundred years ago, you would have had a very different set of social expectations placed upon you. Your social success would be determined by a number of factors, such as how ethically you conducted yourself in business and in family matters and how you related to your friends, neighbors, and relatives. These things were determinative of how well you would get on in life. Treating someone badly, committing adultery, or cheating on your taxes was such a serious breach of community life that you would most likely be shunned into shame by your loved ones. In other words, your social success was directly connected to your character and community involvement.

Such a way of understanding ourselves is almost unimaginable to us today. Back then everyone knew the rules, and their self-understanding came from fitting into a cultural order. Yet these social rules didn't help everyone. If you were of the wrong race, gender, or class, your community might have given you a sense of identity that you didn't exactly want. For the last one hundred years, we have been slowly rejecting the social institutions of our forebears. The dream was for the individual to be truly free from constraining cultural expectations. And for better or worse, we got what we hoped for: today individualism reigns. We no longer look to social institutions and community to find our sense of self; rather, we seek to "be free," to "express ourselves," and to "be happy with ourselves." But how do we achieve these things? We have unprecedented personal freedom, but our freedom is accompanied by a haunting sense of being lost. This sense comes in part from the way we understand our lives today.

To find a real sense of self, to discover who we really are, we first must work out how we got in the position we are in. We must discover the ways in which our sense of self has become infected and unstuck. We must seek to understand how we have moved away from basing our identities in our God-given image and toward simply adopting identities from the culture around us.

CHAPTER 2

From Image of God to Public Image

I n the past, people didn't seem to struggle with the question of identity in the way we do today. Other questions were at the forefront of their minds, and they derived a sense of self from a commonly held standard. We have only to look at church history to see how this is true.

THE IMAGE OF GOD

John Bunyan wrote *Pilgrim's Progress* while imprisoned for his Puritan beliefs in 1678. The book is his spiritual biography told through allegory, and it is considered not only a Christian classic but a classic of English literature. It has been read for centuries by people who are interested in understanding the concept of spiritual growth.

At the beginning of Bunyan's tale, we find the hero of the book, named Christian, in a spiritual depression. Bunyan writes that

Christian is "greatly distressed"; he cries out, "What must I do to be saved?" Bunyan's story has had such resonance with readers since its writing because the character Christian's struggle to find a sense of connection with God, to deal with his guilt and his burden of sin, has been the same struggle of Bunyan's readers. Such concerns about forming a relationship with God and dealing with the personal burden of sin were also foremost on the mind of the young Martin Luther, the father of Protestantism, as he decided to break away from the Roman Catholic Church and begin a new stream of Christianity. You don't have to read much history to see that, for millions of people who have lived in Christian cultures since the birth of the early church, the question of connecting with God and dealing with the burden of sin took precedence over questions of personal identity. This is because people living in Christian cultures in the past believed the book of Genesis when it told them they were created in God's image.

Now, I don't for one second want to paint a sanitized version of the past. Christian cultures have often failed to see the image of God in other cultures and, sadly, sometimes committed abominable actions in the name of Christ; but on the whole, the idea of God-given identity was foundational to a person's sense of self. The belief that humans were created in the image of God was the center point of an understanding of self. It was the cornerstone upon which identity was built.

GREEKS BEARING GOODNESS

Christianity was not the only influence, however, on Western culture. The philosophy of the ancient Greeks also molded the way individuals felt about their lives. The Greeks were obsessed with the ideas of virtue and goodness. The giant of Greek philosophy, Socrates, believed that if humans came to understand what was good, they would act in a way that was good, and therefore their lives would be happy. The Greeks looked to a greater good, an essence or standard of good, to define their lives. Thus, a desire to act in ways that are moral or good is embedded in Western culture, and our identity has been linked closely to our ability to live in a virtuous manner.

THE VERTICAL SELF

This framework of identity, with its Judeo-Christian belief in God-given identity and a Greek belief in virtuous living, can be described as "the vertical self." The vertical self explains the way that identity is developed by being part of a greater order.

At the top of this vertical order is God. Above us, therefore, albeit symbolically, is also a belief in an eternal reward and a greater spiritual reality. Humans develop a sense of self by looking upward, looking to the belief that they are created in God's image to be his ambassadors:

> Then God said, "Let us make human beings in our image, in our likeness, so that they may rule over the fish in the sea and the birds in the sky, over the livestock, and all the wild animals, and over all the creatures that move along the ground."
> So God created human beings in his own image,
> in the image of God he created him;
> male and female he created them.
> God blessed them and said to them, "Be fruitful and increase in number; fill the earth and subdue it. Rule over the fish in the sea and the birds in the sky and over every living creature that moves on the ground." (Gen. 1:26–28)

Humans also look upward to measure their behavior against a greater moral good.

In the middle of this order is earth, creation. Looking downward, humans view creation to see how they are different from it. We see that we have a divine imprint that does not exist in the animal kingdom. However, humans are also challenged to be stewards of creation, to cultivate and tend nature and the environment.

In a realm below nature we find the concepts of eternal punishment for sin, spiritual consequence, and evil. This level reminds us that there are eternal ramifications to our actions in this life, that we have the freedom to accept our God-given identity but we also have the freedom to reject this gift—and to choose a future separate from God with all of the horror that choice brings.

The vertical self is defined by being part of a greater reality. This worldview leads to a belief in the eternal, the desire to cultivate one's spirituality so that one moves upward on the path toward becoming more like God. The vertical self has been the dominant influence on Western culture's understanding of self since the birth of the church. But things have changed.

GOD AS ULTIMATE AUTHORITY

SOUL CONCERN

ETERNAL CONSEQUENCES OF SIN

THE VERTICAL SELF

BLOWING UP THE PAST

A mere nine years after John Bunyan had published *Pilgrim's Progress*, the citizens of Athens found themselves under attack by the navy of Venice. To protect themselves from harm, they hid in their temple, the Parthenon. The temple represented the heights of Greek culture and thought. When Greece converted to Christianity, the temple had been turned into Athens's cathedral. The citizens of Athens thought the Parthenon was a good hiding place because they believed the Venetian invaders would never fire upon this symbol of both Christian piety and the heights of Greek thought. They were wrong. A mortar shell was fired at the temple, and the building became the ruins that we see on tourist postcards today.

Although no one realized it at the time, it was a deeply symbolic moment.[1] For centuries Western culture had looked backward, but now a new period in history had begun. Humans began to look forward; we had entered the modern age. The modern age would create a whirlwind of change that would touch many elements of human existence—especially the way in which we view our lives.

THE LIFE SMOOTHIE

The way you see yourself and understand your identity is not unique. You feel the way you do because you are a product of a culture that has shaped you to process the world in a particular way. If you are to have a life that is rich and rewarding, it is essential that you understand this formation process. No longer do we understand ourselves and our identities through the lens of the vertical self; things have radically shifted. Now the way we see ourselves is the result of a mishmash of influences. It's kind of like a smoothie—all kinds of ingredients and influences have been put into a food processor, the button has been pushed, and everything has been mashed up and served to you as your identity. Without turning this into Sociology 101, let's take a quick tour of the influences that make you see yourself the way you do.

Influence 1: Weird Science

It's hard to imagine that science could have an effect on your identity, but it does. The rise of the modern era was directly linked to the rise of science. The advent of the scientific age affected our view of self in two main ways: First, science is the measurement of what can be ascertained by the five senses; therefore, science began to change the way we perceive the world. Instead of turning to the spiritual, people began to look for answers in what could be sensed or measured. This meant that people began to turn to the material instead of the spiritual when it came to finding a sense of self, and thus we began to move away from the vertical self.

Second, science changed how we view our God-given identity. Humans, in the scientific-materialist worldview, are just another animal, albeit a slightly more advanced species. To see the influence of such a view, you need only watch the Nazi propaganda film that justified the execution of the disabled and the mentally ill by showing images of several chickens pecking to death another chicken that had the misfortune of being born with only one leg. This is an extreme interpretation, but the point is clear: by viewing ourselves not as created in the image of God but as simply another part of the animal kingdom, we moved away from the vertical self and began to perceive our identities in a whole new way. No longer were our identities governed by the laws of the kingdom of God, but rather by the laws of the jungle.

Influence 2: Losing My Religion

On September 4, 1847, the Reverend H. F. Lyte preached his last sermon. Suffering from ill health, he would be dead before the year was out. He left his chapel, which was filled mostly with fishermen, went back to his home, and wrote the classic hymn "Abide with Me." The hymn has provided solace to countless believers. When you consider that ministers like Reverend Lyte feared that the intellectual foundations of their faith were collapsing around them, the hymn takes on a different tone. It is a plea for God to stay with humanity, because religion seemed to be leaving Western culture.[2]

The rise of science and the modern age meant that all religious belief was questioned. The intellectual elites of Europe, tired and dismayed by the religious wars that had set the continent aflame since the Reformation, began to take religion less seriously. By the nineteenth century, people were making the bold prediction that religion would be as dead as the dodo within fifty years. Western cultures shifted from faith in God to faith in our own human potential. The conviction of the day was that humanity would move forward and, through science and reason, create a kind of heaven on earth—minus God. No longer did Western culture look to the heavens to find a sense of self or a God-given identity; instead, it looked to the material world to discover a new way of processing identity.

Influence 3: "I'm Kind of a Big Deal"

A young girl, no more than sixteen, walks past me. She has a confident swagger in her step and wears expensive sunglasses even though she is indoors. She is wearing a T-shirt that reads "I'm kind of a big deal!" She is a classic example of the way radical individualism has shaped our self-identity.

As belief in God-given identity came to be viewed as a superstition of the past and was replaced with an unwavering faith in the potential of humanity's power, a new way of viewing the self was born. It was the dawn of the radical individual. With the influence of the church dissipating and revolutions across Europe and America deposing kings and aristocracies, the individual became the new ruler of his or her world. No longer did people find their identities dictated by church, king, class, or state. The rise of democracies meant that the individual defined his or her own identity and place in the world. Never before had the individual been so free, but that freedom came with a massive price tag—our sense of self.

Influence 4: Making It

As I waited at a café one day, I noticed a young woman hunched over a thick book. She was taking notes. I wondered what she was reading, because she wore a look of deep concentration. So intense was her focus and almost prayerful devotion to the material she was studying, I wondered if she might be reading the Bible or a New Age book or maybe something by the Dalai Lama. Unable to control my curiosity, I went to the counter to grab a superfluous packet of sugar and get a closer look. She was not reading the Bible; she was reading the writings of another guru of our day and age, Donald Trump. She was being discipled by one of the great streams that informs our sense of self: the achievement identity.

In the entire scheme of history, such a view of personhood is relatively new. Its genesis can be found during the years our culture moved from an agricultural basis to an industrial one. In order to find work, family members were forced to move away from each other. Once isolated, these individuals found it harder to be the object of shame, since relatives didn't know what they were up to. Also, in a big city it was much harder for neighbors to know the ins and outs of each other's private lives. A person could have an affair with someone across town and no one would know. The anonymity afforded by urban living began to change how people lived.

As factories sprang up and people moved from rural environments to urban ones, it didn't matter whether you were of good character. What began to matter instead was how well you could operate the machinery in the factory. The bottom line of profit started to take over the former defining line of personal virtue. A person's function became more important than his or her character. People needed to be levelheaded, not swayed by emotions; after all, when one's function in a larger social machine is paramount, feelings and sentimentality get in the way. Being good at tasks and functions was valued more than simply being good. Our ability to produce began to define our identity.

Someone who worked hard, who had ambition, talent, education, and sheer determination, could "make it." Making it meant, of course, moving up a peg in the social order. For centuries European culture had kept people in a system they could not break free from (based on landowners, farmers, artisans, and the aristocracy). But now people could work hard to move up the ladder of social status. Culture started telling us that we could find identity through what we did and what we achieved.

Influence 5: Cheesy Love Songs . . . Well, Sort Of

Not everyone was happy to be just another cog in the new industrial social machine, so a countercultural voice began to speak of a different way to be human, a new way of understanding self. Novels, paintings, and plays called for a different way of understanding ourselves, one based not purely on our functions and abilities, but rather on our feelings, passions, desires, and emotions. This backlash against a mechanical view of life encouraged people to look deep inside the personal interior world—the world of feelings, of instinct, of emotions. It encouraged people to seek experiences, to find meaning in romantic love. It glorified foreign cultures and travel; it deified creativity and art. It urged people to look outside the Judeo-Christian faith for spiritual inspiration from nature or even from other religions and spiritualities. By following this romantic countercultural movement, we hoped to find a new true understanding of self in the shadow of a mechanical, industrial culture. This influence on how we see ourselves is still deeply felt today. We see it again and again in the stories told by our popular culture. We see it in our desire to travel and gain experiences. We observe it in our desire to sample and taste various cultures.

The mechanical and the romantic visions of self still run parallel to each other in the lives of people today. They still influence much of our understanding of self. For example, our society worships romantic love. Songs, movies, and novels all speak of romantic love being the most important thing in life. We are told that when we fall in love, we will "find ourselves." But the fluid twenty-first-century culture in which we live requires us to move often, to not commit, to resist things that may get in the way of production, so we are becoming less and less committed to relationships. We end up in the ludicrous position of wanting to be in a loving relationship but doing everything we can to undermine our chances of having one. We are in conflict with ourselves. We struggle to find a sense of self that is complete.

THE VERTICAL SELF IN TATTERS

The combination of these influences means that you are born into a culture in which the vertical self is shattered. As the twentieth century began, the wheels began to fall off the dream of progress. The carnage of World War I, the economic crisis of the Great Depression, and the failure of communism's Utopian dreams all began to chip away at humanity's faith in progress. Nothing, however, can illustrate this collapse in confidence in our Western culture more clearly than the Holocaust, in which more than six million Jewish people and other minorities were put to death by one of Europe's supposedly most progressive and civilized cultures.

A collective bout of anxiety fell over the West as our foundations began to crack. All of a sudden people began to question what had gone wrong. Nothing was safe from suspicion or questioning. The deconstruction of the religious sense of self was complete. Any sense of identity, any concept of self, began to be viewed with suspicion and skepticism. A crucial move had been made in Western culture: we moved away from a vertical understanding of self to one that could be described as horizontal.

THE RISE OF THE HORIZONTAL SELF

In a secular culture drenched in a worldview of suspicion, the individual cannot look higher than the self with any degree of certainty. Thus, religion, spirituality, tradition, and culture cannot tell a wider story that offers the individual a sense of place and meaning. The secular individual can only look sideways— hence the contrasting term *horizontal self*. Looking sideways does not give one a wider story to believe. The horizontal self looks to others for a sense of identity rather than to something larger than oneself, thus finding a sense of self in one's status within society. With God playing no real authoritative role in informing identity, people look to others as the ultimate judge. Whereas the vertical self looks to heaven for favor and approval, the horizontal self looks to the world for approval and acceptance. For people who hold a horizontal sense of self, the creation and cultivation of a public image are paramount.

Peers and society act as a mirror: we look to them to gain a sense of identity, yet they can only relay back to us the messages that we communicate to them. You cannot describe yourself as cool. Others must label you cool. In that way our identities are dependent on what others think of us. However, this means we do not think of others as being created in the image of God. We turn them into mirrors with one purpose—to tell us who we are. They are our audience. Whereas people with a vertical sense of self look to their God-given identity to find a sense of self, those with a horizontal sense of self can only hope that they will project the right image into culture so they will receive the right messages back from their peers. Therefore, even the shy are drawn into the constant pursuit of putting out a public image, of running a personal public relations campaign in order to receive messages of meaning. It doesn't matter what you really think or feel; all that matters is what people see.

People with a vertical sense of self look beyond their earthly lives to eternity to see the continued development of their identities, but the horizontal self is forced to look only at the temporary. The idea of eternity is constrained to the world of immediacy that the horizontal self creates. This immediacy results in the notion that a pleasure you have to wait for is not worth it.

The British actor Michael Palin commented after journeying across the Sahara Desert with several nomadic tribes that he could see why Judaism, Christianity, and Islam came out of the desert. He found that the experience of walking for days and days with only sand before his eyes sent him inward to confront his spirituality, his understanding of God, and his inner self. But we live in a world of constant distraction and buzz, thus avoiding the journey inward, living only on the surface of life, concerned only with the external.

With no understanding beyond the immediate, with no grasp of eternal spiritual realities, the horizontal self sees no point in spiritual growth. Instead, it develops a public self, and publicity takes precedence over spiritual growth. With no greater goal, significance is milked out of fleeting moments.

The horizontal self is faced with a desperate burden to create or find identity during *this* life. Those with a horizontal view must ensure that they keep communicating the right messages to their peers and society at large. For them, "sin" is not fitting in; "hell" is social irrelevance. With no larger truth present in their worldview, truth and facts mean little. Instead, they look for identity in momentary pleasure and experience. As the horizontal self sabotages our chances of finding our true selves, identity is exchanged for imagery. It is a profoundly different way of existing as a human being.

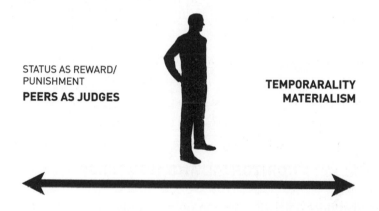

STATUS AS REWARD/
PUNISHMENT
PEERS AS JUDGES

**TEMPORARALITY
MATERIALISM**

THE HORIZONTAL SELF

Vertical Self	Horizontal Self
God as judge	Others as judge
Holiness	Status
Eternal	Temporary
Delayed gratification	Instant gratification
Work ethic	Play ethic

Vertical Self	Horizontal Self
Growth	Experiential
Character	Attitude
Identity	Image
Humility	Publicity
I	Me
Sin	Boredom/irrelevance
Contribution	Achievement
Goal	Journey
Satisfaction	Momentary pleasure
Wholeness	Fragmentation
Faith	Skepticism
Self-discipline	Self-esteem
Communal	Individual
Inner life	Outer appearance
Engagement	Distraction
Facts	Feelings

HORIZONTAL AND HOMELESS

With a horizontal view, we can only look to media and our peers for a sense of self, so it is no wonder that we constantly find ourselves confused when it comes to discovering our identities. When it comes to our identities, it is as if we are now homeless. The vertical self provided a home for our identities that was secure and stable. But now our identities are unsheltered, subject to the elements, to passing cultural fads and the opinions of our peers. We desire to find a home, a place where we can be accepted and loved unconditionally for who we are, but the age of the horizontal self means that we must keep on the move, constantly trying to play by our culture's rules of identity and constant competition with those around us for attention and affection.

CHAPTER 3

Finding Yourself

Being an office supplies store manager is not what Dale expected to be. He hates having to explain what he does to other people at parties. He wishes he had a job he could be proud of. He has just left his role as a youth cell group leader after six years. He isn't sure why, but it just didn't seem to "do it" for him anymore. Part of the reason may be that Dale realizes he is a different person when he is with different people. He knows that he is sometimes Christian Dale, sometimes Party Dale, sometimes Depressed Dale. Charming Dale knows that he has the ability to impress girls, but as soon as he gets into a relationship, he turns into Insecure Dale, and the relationship falls apart. Sometimes when he is listening to music or drinking with his friends, everything in life feels good. But other times Dale finds himself alone in his bedroom, yelling, swearing, and wanting to break things. Dale has started lifting weights; maybe if he looks ripped, he will feel better.

Dale's story illustrates that we have now entered a new age of anxiety about who we are. Any solid ground upon which to build an identity is in doubt. The horizontal self places the incredible burden of finding and forging an identity upon the individual. We find ourselves in situations of constant self-questioning and self-examination. Our cultural climate dictates that all truths must be questioned, so with no truth to hold on to and any Utopian dreams of changing our culture in tatters, all that is left are interior feelings, the distraction of romantic love, and the lure of pleasurable experiences. With good character and personal virtue things of the past, and with no agreed-upon cultural values on which to build an identity, those who maintain a horizontal sense of self must then find themselves. They must discover who they are, but with no solid ground. The rules of the game keep changing. And so, to discover a sense of identity, individuals must constantly reinvent themselves.

RECONSTRUCTING YOUR IDENTITY

Youri's family is Armenian-American. He grew up in a suburb filled with Armenians. The Armenian community was a huge part of his youth. It seemed that a wedding took place every weekend, church was held every Sunday, and visits and meals with distant relatives happened nonstop. As a teenager, Youri could not skateboard behind the mall without one of his aunts or an older woman from the community complaining to his mother that he was hanging around, causing trouble. After college, Youri moved to a hip inner-city precinct about an hour away from where he grew up. He loves his new neighborhood and finally feels free now that he is away from the constant scrutiny of people in his Armenian community. Where he lives now, people are more interested in what music he is listening to than whether he is dating an Armenian girl. Deep down he loves the fact that his mother hates his tattoos and piercings. Sometimes, however, he finds himself missing his family and the familiarity that came with walking around the neighborhood and having everyone know his name.

The change in Youri's self-image reflects the way people today attempt to change their lives by changing their identities. Constantly changing your image is key to maintaining a public life. For years now, celebrities—particularly musicians like David Bowie and Madonna—have reinvented themselves time and time again to prolong their careers, enforcing the idea that a change in hair color, different clothes, or a new sound makes you a new person. Celebrities pioneer the trends that millions imitate.

The Sydney Harbor Bridge is probably one of the most well-known landmarks in Australia. Each year visitors climb the bridge to gain a stunning view of Sydney's downtown and harbor. The sheer size of the bridge means that the structure is constantly being repainted. As soon as the painters finish, they have to start again at the other end. Such is the task.

Our identities today are constantly being remade. As soon as one public persona is mastered, it becomes out of date. In the age of the horizontal self, the reconstruction of our identities is normal. Whole industries are built around offering people various ways to reinvent themselves. Reinvention is not just encouraged in our culture; it is demanded. We are told that to not reinvent ourselves is to not stay relevant. I spoke to a group of college students recently, and they said that the biggest pressure they have in their lives is to "keep up"—keep up with the right look, the right music, and the right technologies. Many in the group shared with me that they were overwhelmed by the pressure of keeping up. They desperately wanted to just give up, but the fear of social isolation was too much, so they gave in to constant reinvention.

People are increasingly spending more and more time honing, changing, and developing public personas. People will also reconstruct their identities when they feel that their lives are not heading in the right direction. By shedding parts or the whole of their identities, they feel that they are shedding the problems they are facing. Think of it this way: when you play a computer game and your character dies, you have the option to simply start all over again. Changing your identity becomes a way of pressing the reset button of life.

It is no surprise that as we find that we can reinvent ourselves and reconstruct our identities, we start inventing different personalities for different situations. Our identities become more fluid, and we find ourselves becoming fragmented.

MANY ME

Dawn has been attending a contemporary charismatic church for more than four years. She loves her friends there and particularly enjoys the worship. She also likes the strong teaching, which she believes has a real biblical basis. For more than eight months now, she has played keyboards in the worship band. She cannot imagine her life without God. When she feels down or lonely, she plays worship songs, and as soon as she starts to play, she feels God's presence and often speaks in tongues.

Dawn has been dating her boyfriend, Dean, for two years. For the first two weeks they did not sleep together (according to their pastor's wishes), but then they decided that was not practical. Dawn has never had a boyfriend with whom she has not had sex. To be abstinent is unthinkable to her; sex is just something she has always been interested in. She keeps this side of her life secret from her two best friends at church, with whom she is in an accountability group. Dawn believes she doesn't need to tell them because she is just "wired differently" than they are, and besides, she wonders to herself, *Why would God want to stop me from having pleasure?*

Dawn's life is a classic example of the way people today can project different personalities in different situations, even subscribing to viewpoints that are contradictory. Dawn simply ditched the traditional Christian teachings on sexuality because they did not suit her "lifestyle." We are confronted daily with an avalanche of competing messages from our families, our peers, our workplaces, the wider community, the media, and our culture. We receive conflicting messages about who we are and who we should be. With no real center to build an identity around, we find these competing messages moving us toward personal fragmentation. We have multiple images for the multiple situations in which we find ourselves. The compartmentalization that began in the age of commuting is exacerbated in our age of the Internet and cheap travel. We spend so much time compartmentalized that we no longer know which of our many selves is our true self. And we fear we may never get back to our true nature again.

A classic case of the fragmentation of self can be found in the media coverage of Michael Jackson's life and death. In remembering his life, the media referred to different Michael Jacksons. There was the supertalented young boy of the Jackson 5; there was the young adult Michael Jackson of the *Off the Wall* and *Thriller* albums; there was the eccentric but lovable Michael Jackson of the early days of the Neverland ranch period. But then there was the seemingly darker and apparently more disturbed Michael Jackson who went on trial and who dangled his baby off a balcony. And there was the reclusive Michael Jackson of the last few years of his life.

People who knew Michael Jackson would talk about "the Michael Jackson I knew" alluding to the fact that there seemed to be different Michael Jacksons. When Jackson died, some of my friends told me that they were mourning the Jackson 5 boy Michael Jackson or the *Thriller* Michael Jackson but not the later Michael Jackson. All the while, everyone seemed to forget that were discussing one man, not many. This phenomenon illuminates the way our media culture seems to split us into different selves.

The Internet has only furthered this breakdown between our real selves and our acting selves. We have now mastered the art of adapting to multiple self-images depending on our circumstances. The anonymity of the Internet allows one to easily be several people, sometimes at the same time. Hiding behind our computer screens, we can become anything we want, leaving our inhibitions behind.

Increasingly people are choosing to live large portions of their lives as alternate online characters, but even more fascinating is the fact that millions more do so in their everyday, real-world lives, putting on and taking off identities like clothing. Vacations are a classic example of this phenomenon. Just look at the advertisements for Las Vegas, which tell us, "What happens in Vegas stays in Vegas!" This slogan indicates that people who enter the city can act in ways they normally wouldn't if they were in their hometown—the implication being that the individual's usual moral code is on a temporary suspension. While people are in Sin City, they can live out a different personality; they can wear a different identity.

Christians also take off and put on different identities in different places. One can have an evangelical Christian worldview, a secular sex life, an economic rationalist approach to money, a conservative vote, and a liberal approach to humor. However, while we may become adept at holding together so many divergent beliefs and personalities, the strain is most certainly felt. Psychologist Kenneth J. Gergen has labeled this breakdown into multiple selves and multiple commitments *multiphrenia*.[1] Theologians Richard Middleton and Brian Walsh point out that in many ways this contemporary phenomenon of multiphrenia bears a strong connection to Jesus' encounter of the demoniac in the gospel of Mark: "When we search for a biblical analogy to multiphrenia, the demon-possessed man of Mark 5 comes to mind . . . 'My name is Legion, for we are many.' . . . Controlled by many spirits, the man in the biblical story was tormented, homeless, and in need of healing. So, it seems to us, is the contemporary, postmodern psyche."[2] We have much in common, then, with Legion, a man tormented by hundreds of demons, a man torn apart by multiple identities and entities. Multiphrenia does not bring us any closer to wholeness. Instead, we are fragmented, our identity smashed in pieces.

OPINION OVER ACTION

Brian is angry about the destruction of the environment. He often finds himself at parties, passionately sharing his opinion with someone about how the government can improve its environmental policies. Brian tells everyone within earshot of his hatred for the oil-guzzling lifestyles of the rich. Brian is particularly livid with the oil companies, whom he sees as the main perpetrators of global warming. On his guitar case he has a sticker that reads "Oil = Death." For eight months Brian has been saving money to spend a year backpacking around the world with four of his college buddies. He recently read that avoiding air travel is one of the best ways to limit the use of fossil fuels and help the environment. But there is no way Brian is canceling his trip; it will be too much fun.

When we have multiple self-images, we find ourselves with conflicting values and views. Because we have retreated to a culture based on publicity and the acting out of multiple identities, our moral choices do not matter. What does matter is being seen as having the right opinions. Instead of letting our actions show our convictions, we speak empty platitudes through our blogs, bumpers stickers, and T-shirt slogans. In the age of the horizontal self, backing up our opinions with the right behavior is seen as neither essential nor necessary. Because there is no authoritative story or deeper set of values, people are quite comfortable holding contradictory opinions within themselves. For hundreds of years the concept of holiness and sin in Western culture created a concern for doing good, for maintaining integrity. Today, however, we are not bothered when our actions do not match our rhetoric. This is because our basic understanding of what it means to be good has changed. It is not as important that we *are* good as it is that we *appear* good.

CONTEMPORARY SAINTS OF GOODNESS

Our greatest scorn is reserved for those who fail at the game of looking good. This is why we have become so obsessed with hypocrisy. We experience a guilty pleasure when others are "found out." We love to see the public fall of ministers struggling with sexual sin, politicians convicted of corruption, television psychologists acting like spoiled brats, and girl-next-door actresses with drug addictions. We chide them for being caught, for not being able to keep up the game of illusion. We deride them for being bad actors. Their charades just prove to us that no one is really good; therefore, we all must just put on an act that says we are. So instead of aiming to be good people, we now aim to be good at things—good at playing tennis, good at making authentic Spanish food, good at performing in bed.[3] We no longer describe ordinary people as good; instead, we reserve that description for the celebrity saints of our culture—people such as Nelson Mandela, Mother Teresa, or the Dalai Lama. Their celebrity is wrapped up in their perceived goodness, and their goodness seems almost otherworldly. We have started to believe that the ordinary person cannot be good, or rather cannot be bothered by being good. So we no longer try. We live with the contradiction. Being good seems to imply that the fun of life is over. Instead, experimenting with goals, dreams, experiences, and personas becomes the responsibility of all individuals trying to find their true selves. The measuring stick for our success in this quest becomes our personal feelings. Do we feel great? Do we feel free? Do we feel happy?

FEELING GOOD

Jimmy is all about partying, and he loves the fact that he has a reputation for being a party animal. He is the first to arrive and the last to leave. His ability to drink is incredible. Jimmy is all about the rush, the buzz, the vibe. He would describe himself as an adrenaline junkie. He is famous among his friends for never turning down a dare, no matter how dangerous. If Jimmy had a philosophy of life, it would be "Feel good all the time": in his opinion there is not much in life worth doing other than having sex, getting high, and partying.

There are millions of people like Jimmy around the world. In the absence of a story or foundation that gives hope or meaning, life has become a never-ending quest for pleasure and experience. Instead of being good, people want to feel good. When people don't feel good, they believe something is wrong in their lives. Cultural commentators have noted that therapy and counseling have become a kind of surrogate religion in the Western world. One of the key components of therapy is that it removes any objective moral claims and instead focuses on the subjective feelings of the client.

Thus, today, with no real agreed-upon values against which to measure our identity and character, we measure our lives by our personal feelings. Millions of us around the world do this. But feelings are fleeting, and the situations that cause good feelings can change. We each remain captive to situations and circumstances that are out of our control; therefore, the individual remains lost. Without the media telling us who we are, we have almost no real sense of personhood left anymore. We do not look to God for a sense of self. Rather, we look inside and find very little, and thus we become obsessed with cultivating our image.

LIFE AS IMAGERY

With no real culturally accepted inner values to work toward, the whole of society has moved toward imagery and publicity. We have all become players in the field of public relations. Just think of politics. Someone who intends to run for public office cannot do so today without a carefully orchestrated public relations campaign. Candidates must learn how to control their words, mannerisms, and displays of emotion in such a way as to communicate their intended messages. Moreover, any past indiscretions they have committed must be covered up. They must be made to look as if they are the sort of candidate the public wants to elect—for example, the family-values advocate, the patriot, or the political maverick. All the while, the real person is hidden behind a false media mask.

Just think of President Bill Clinton, complete with sunglasses, playing his saxophone on *The Arsenio Hall Show*, evoking various cultural and media images of cool, sexy, and hip. When I first saw the images of President Bush announcing the end of the war in Iraq, in his flight suit, I instantly thought of Tom Cruise's character Maverick in the film *Top Gun*.[4] The line between reality and entertainment has become blurred. The people our culture tells us we should look to and emulate offer us no help in discovering our authentic selves; instead, we only find media mask after media mask. This effect extends outside of politics; our own lives have become exercises in public relations as we struggle to project the right image.

PROJECTING A SUCCESSFUL IMAGE

Living in the age of the horizontal self, in which our worth is tied to what others think of us, we end up obsessed with ourselves. We are always thinking of ways to hone our act, our public persona, our looks and grooming. We are narcissistic and obsessive about our own appearance and public brand, and the opinions of others are supreme to us. Therefore, we find it essential to cast a winning persona, and when everything is a competition, we must show others that we are doing well. We are told that we must be confident; we must give off the right image or attitude. The challenge, though, is that many of us deep down do not feel confident. No problem! If you cannot pull off the confident act, you can simply hire a confidence coach who will show you, through the use of body language, grooming, and assertiveness, how to project a successful image even if you do not feel that way on the inside. But a vicious cycle is born: the more you place your public persona under the microscope, the more insecure you become. You notice your physical flaws; you notice personality traits you are unhappy with. You also begin to notice the positive attributes others have that you do not possess. I saw an interview with a well-known international model in which the interviewer commented that it must be wonderful to be so beautiful. The model responded that it wasn't wonderful, because she was constantly in magazines, on billboards, and in advertisements, and she was stuck in a state of constant self-evaluation. Every flaw was magnified (often on giant billboards) because she was such a public figure. She felt entrapped. Others saw a beautiful woman, but she saw only her flaws. Often, the better we are at projecting a winning attitude, the more tension we feel between our public self and the reality of our broken humanity.

But if we don't feel like projecting a winning image—if we feel we are too messed up—we can simply project a broken image. Much of youth culture has been built around this kind of non-winning attitude. Just think of the high school goth kid, slowly shuffling around, wearing supposedly antisocial clothes, listening to deliberately depressive music. On one hand, he seems to be rejecting the projection of the social self; he is nothing like those around him who are trying to impress others with their success and attractiveness. However, if you look deeper, you find that he is doing just the same thing as them. The cheerleader who has chosen the social image of "popular" is really no different from the goth teenager who has chosen the social image of "outcast." Both are engaged in a public performance in which the social signals they send to their audience are of supreme importance to their personal understanding of self. They are sending out different messages, but both are just as tied to the messages that they get back.

"I ♥ ME!" THE NEW NARCISSISM

One of our secular culture's responses to our identity crisis is to try to create a value-free sense of self, one that is not linked to any sense of truth outside of the individual. We see this most clearly in the self-esteem message so prevalent in our culture. The 1980s saw a radical shift in education across much of the Western world, in which the pass/fail mode of competency was replaced by an emphasis on self-esteem and positive self-worth. A number of psychologists have, upon reflection, criticized this emphasis on imposed self-esteem, linking it to a rise in arrogance, self-obsession, and a lack of empathy among young adults who were educated in the 1980s and 1990s. Because the self-esteem message is not linked to any wider story or truth other than the mantra "We are all special," it carries little weight in informing our sense of self beyond simply inflating our egos.

As psychologist Jean Twenge notes, "Self-esteem without basis encourages laziness . . . True self-confidence comes from honing your talents and learning things, not from being told you're great just because you exist . . . Building up the self-esteem and importance of children who are already egocentric can bring trouble, as it can lead to narcissism."[5] The term *narcissism* is derived from the Greek myth of Narcissus, who was so self-obsessed that he stared too long at his own reflection in a lake and fell in and drowned. The cultural critic Christopher Lasch—in his best-selling book, *The Culture of Narcissism*[6]—wrote that with the decline of religion in the West, narcissism has become the dominant identity or personality of our time. In many ways narcissism is an arrogant insecurity; it is another symptom of our lack of self. The rise of the narcissistic personality is another pointer to our need for a renewed understanding of self. Twenge describes the traits of a narcissistic personality:

> Narcissists are overly focused on themselves and lack empathy for others, which means that they cannot see another person's perspective . . . They also feel entitled to special privileges and believe that they are superior to other people. As a result, narcissists are bad relationship partners and can be difficult to work with. Narcissists are also more likely to be hostile, feel anxious, compromise their health, and fight with friends and family.[7]

Many of the traits of narcissism are encouraged in our culture today. Just think of the millions of hours people across the world now spend cultivating their online identities on sites such as Facebook, Twitter, and MySpace, tweaking the images and identities they wish to broadcast to the world. Never before has humanity spent such an inordinate amount of time making ourselves look good. Today we do not even blink at such narcissism; it has become a lynchpin of youth culture. Doing such a thing even ten years ago would have meant being shunned or at least thought of as arrogant.

A youth pastor told me recently that she couldn't get the students in her college group to read one Bible verse a week. They complained that they didn't have the time. Yet when she looked at their social networking Web sites, she estimated that on average her students were spending half an hour to two hours a night updating and maintaining their Internet public profile. In the media-drenched landscape in which we live, vanity is no longer a sin; it is a virtue. Narcissism is no longer a psychological condition; it is now celebrated. Narcissists are encouraged as they are complimented for having confidence or "attitude."

PERSONAL LOSTNESS

We are paralyzed by not knowing who we really are. Instead of having well-defined identities, we have a churning sea of conflicting feelings and desires inside us. When we don't know who we are, we find it hard to know what we should be doing. We may have the right qualifications, we may have the skills and talent, but often we fear we will make the wrong decisions about our futures.

When we don't know who we are, we become slaves to our feelings. The momentary emotions that we feel begin to dominate our lives, and we become what we are feeling in that moment. When we don't know who we are, we become entrapped by circumstance. The world defines us, our lives become reactive to whatever is happening around us, and we become more and more frustrated as the ups and downs of life govern us. We become confused. We find that we're struggling with ourselves. We give up trying to find out who we are, and instead we act. We treat life as if it were a movie—our disposable identities are the roles that we play. We look to the media to provide those identities.

Life, the Movie

M onths and months have gone into the preparation. Parents have contributed tens of thousands of dollars. The church has been transformed—no longer is it a simple suburban chapel; it now looks like something from a movie. The bride has undergone a transformation too; she has tanned, lost weight, and gotten Hollywood hair and makeup. Her friends drool over her dress. It is copied down to the last detail from a dress featured in a recent celebrity magazine's wedding issue. As the vintage luxury car pulls up to the church, the bride surveys the gathering crowd: everyone is here to see her. She looks at her wedding planner with a sense of relief as he directs the proceedings.

She steps out of the car and is met by a barrage of camera flashes—her family and friends acting as paparazzi. She cannot help but beam as she overhears her friends commenting on how stunning she looks. *The day is finally here*, she thinks to herself, feeling like a princess as a thousand media memories course through her mind, from Princess Diana's wedding to countless romantic comedies and Disney princess films. The professional wedding video camera crew motions that it's time to head inside. Her bridesmaid grasps her hand and leads her to the chapel, whispering in her ear, "This is your day. You are the star."

Welcome to life as a movie. In the past the bride and groom were merely bit players in a community event. But approximately twenty years ago that changed, and weddings became more about the wants and desires of the bride and groom. Today they are full-blown media events in which the lines between entertainment and real life become blurred. They are now about delivering a celebrity-for-a-day experience—attempting to bring the mythology of the movies into everyday life. And this is not just happening with weddings.

The primary lens through which the average citizen of the Western world views his or her life and identity is the cinema. Life is now a movie. This is the contention of media theorist Neal Gabler and is spelled out in his stunning and deeply perceptive book *Life: The Movie*.[1] Cinema has replaced religion as the primary way in which we understand our lives; the medium of film has profoundly changed how we view ourselves and our identities. Gabler writes of the way that people now view their lives through the lens of movies: "Personal life movies, billions of them, starring ordinary people . . . were playing in everyday existence: on the street, at the office or factory, at a restaurant or shopping mall or local bar, in school, at a party, in the living room, even in the bedroom."[2] This has become the age of the performing self, who is always, as they say in showbiz, "on."

If the vertical self honors character and the development of an inner self, the horizontal self, with its emphasis on public image, naturally elevates performance above character. Historian Warren Susman writes, "The social role demanded of all in the new culture of personality was that of a performer. Every American was to become a performing self."[3] Without anyone other than a few observant sociologists and media theorists noticing that our sense of self has radically shifted, we no longer find a sense of self through the art of living. Instead, we find a sense of self through performance. We no longer live; we act. We have all become actors in the movies of our lives.

In the past, the line between the stage and the audience was a clear one. People understood that actors on the stage were portraying characters who were part of a choreographed act. Once the actors took off their makeup and costumes, they shed the roles they were playing and returned to their everyday lives. Everyone understood the rules of the game. Theater was entertainment, an escape from the drudgery of everyday working life. The theater was simply a couple of hours to escape to a fantasy world, an occasional treat. But now the line separating the stage and the audience is hazy. The dawn of the "celebrity" was part of the problem. As actors became more and more famous, the roles they played onstage began to blur with their actual lives. Those watching in the audience were so bewitched with the fantasy that they wanted it to continue once the curtain dropped. The fantasy was too powerful, too attractive. The advent of cinema was key in destroying the line between stage and real life.

LIFE ON THE RED CARPET

The average person has virtually no chance of bumping into an A-list Hollywood actor. The only real exposure we have to celebrities' real lives is through paparazzi shots featured in gossip magazines. These blurry photos taken from a distance have the same effect as those fuzzy images you see of supposed UFOs, Sasquatch, or the Loch Ness monster. They just heighten the mystique and mystery, contributing to further blurring between acting and real life.

We also see actors offstage on that otherworldly plane known as the red carpet. Any illusion that we are glimpsing the real selves of Hollywood stars is destroyed when we watch their behavior closely. The Hollywood starlet will sometimes spend days preparing for a red carpet appearance. Normally a whole team will go into action, guiding her through a process of dieting, exercising, choosing the right dress, taping the dress into place, and styling her makeup and hair. It is a major preproduction. The combined effect of this makeover is that the starlet looks very different than she does in her normal, everyday life.

The starlet arrives at the red carpet in a limousine—always. The limousine is a cultural sign that things are not normal. Apart from prom night or a wedding, the average person will never ride in a limousine. Limousines indicate that we have left the real world of normality, that behind the tinted windows is someone abnormally important. As the starlet steps out of the limousine, we are reminded by the assembled media and the starlet's entourage that we are not watching something average. Most fascinatingly, as we see the starlet walk up the carpet, we notice that she is behaving in an unusual way. Every few steps she stops to pose in particular predetermined ways she has learned.

These particular poses serve a couple of purposes. First, they accentuate the actress's positive physical features. For example, you will see her put one foot forward to give the illusion of height; you will also see her turn her shoulders at right angles to her waist so as to give the appearance of a smaller waist. Another popular pose is with her back to the cameras but with her head turned to look back over her shoulder. This pose is a powerful piece of body language, one that appeals to men at a deeply sexual, physiological level. The more we watch, we realize that although the starlets are not performing in a play, movie, or television program, they are still acting.

We experience the same phenomenon when we watch celebrities being interviewed. The polite and smiling actor is engaged in the act of public relations, of putting on a public face that will encourage us to go and view his movie. As we watch, however, we ask ourselves, *Is the actor presenting his real self or a carefully crafted public self?* We think back to the 1950s heartthrob who was actually gay. We think of the clean-cut actor who was actually a cocaine addict. Or we think of the comedian who struggled with depression. I remember, after Tom Cruise's famous jumping-on-the-couch incident on *The Oprah Winfrey Show*, overhearing my friends debating whether his enthusiasm over his new relationship was genuine or rather a carefully orchestrated piece of public relations. People asked whether that was the real Tom Cruise or just an act.

I remember seeing an interview with a singer who had just released a highly sexually provocative music video. The interviewer asked her if she was really as sexual as she was in her performances. The singer laughed and said that when she was onstage or on film, that was just her "sexy" character. She shared that she was nothing like her public persona and actually preferred to lounge around at home in her track pants. While she understood clearly the difference between her public persona and her real self, I am sure that the millions of young girls who buy her singles are not so aware of the difference.

All celebrities are actors now, whether they make a living acting or not. Just look at the way pro athletes conduct themselves. Media theorist Thomas de Zengotita, in his book *Mediated*,[4] notes that professional athletes now act. They are no longer just sports people. Observe the way they celebrate, the way they play to the crowd. Even the crowd acts, becoming part of the spectacle, part of the performance.

We often see athletes, famous entrepreneurs, or singers appearing in a movie or television show as themselves. Even stranger is the phenomenon seen in television shows like *Entourage*, which features actors playing themselves in fictional stories. They are actors acting as if they are not acting, yet they really *are* acting. Work that one out. Again we find the line between the stage and the audience blurred, the line between acting and our authentic selves confused. We can see now why celebrities and celebrity culture have become a big influence on our understanding of self.

WE ARE ALL STARS NOW

I remember seeing the power of celebrity when I watched soccer player David Beckham's first game in the American Major League Soccer for his new team, the Los Angeles Galaxy. Beckham had been injured a few weeks earlier and began the game on the bench. It didn't take long to realize that the actual game was merely a side event to the celebrity showcase that was David Beckham. The camera kept switching between the actual game and Beckham sitting on the bench; the crowd in the stadium and the millions watching around the world seemed to be more interested in Beckham's reactions to what was happening than in the game itself. Throughout the telecast, the coverage would break away from the game to show the various celebrities in the crowd who had come to pay homage to Beckham. The organizers had even set up a red carpet leading into the stadium for the various celebrities who attended, reinforcing the celebrity power of the event. The irony is that most soccer experts agree that Beckham is not the best player in history. He is not even close! But his celebrity status eclipses his playing ability. The celebrity is given almost superhuman abilities by our culture. In fact, one advertisement for Beckham's fragrance has him appearing godlike in a desert, the clouds and weather moving around him at his whim. This is the power of celebrity.

Sociologist Chris Rojek observes in his book *Celebrity* that celebrity culture has become a dominant force in our society due to three main influences.[5] First, our culture has moved from an aristocratic culture, in which people achieved status simply by being born into the right family, to a democratic culture, in which we are told that with dedication, hard work, and talent, anyone (even those from the lowliest stations in life) can be propelled to the heights of fame and social status. Today you don't even need to have a particular skill or talent; you just have to be in the right place at the right time to, as our culture says, "make it." Consequently, the prospect of celebrity, particularly for youth and young adults, appears far away but also tantalizingly close. Rojek also notes that one can become famous today by becoming notorious. Many serial killers, terrorists, and perpetrators of public massacres have spoken of the desire to be known, to make an impression—revealing fame as their motive when they are captured, through suicide notes, or on posthumous video postings. The cultural lure of celebrity is so strong that many are prepared to gain fame by notoriety.[6]

Second, Rojek notes that celebrity has grown as religion has declined in the Western world. Without gods, saints, or shamans, our culture looks to celebrities to inject a sense of mystique and otherworldliness into what we see as the routine of our ordinary lives. Look at the way the crowd at a rock concert screams and swoons, almost in the way that people from tribal cultures move during religious rituals. Ordinary people will swoon and even faint upon meeting celebrities. Pieces of hair, used coffee cups, clothes, and even bodily fluids from celebrities are sold for huge sums online. The buyer subconsciously attempts to access the celebrity's power by connecting to him or her through a tangible item. This phenomenon is very similar to the Christian pilgrimages during the Middle Ages to sites that claimed to possess artifacts or relics that once belonged to saints. The pilgrim hoped to gain a blessing by coming into the relic's proximity. Thus, Rojek reflects that "celebrity culture provides an important integrating function in secular society."[7] This function is that the lives of celebrities—their adventures and misadventures—offer a shared experience in which people can find common ground with others.

Third, Rojek astutely notes that the rise of celebrity culture is linked to the commodification of everyday life, which is a fancy way of saying that everything now is a product to be consumed. Thus, our culture creates celebrities by turning ordinary people into stylized images of our deepest wants and desires. The famous serial killer plays the role of the person we love to hate and fear. The sex symbol becomes the ultimate image of our sexual fantasies and desires. The famous computer entrepreneur becomes the embodiment of our desire to move beyond our station in life. And the much-loved TV host becomes the image of our desire for a perfect parent figure.

Celebrities play a key role in our culture today. They offer a framework for how we should behave. As with the saints of the Middle Ages, their lives are held up to be emulated. The culture of the celebrity also deeply influences those who are not famous. It deeply shapes our sense of self. Rojek observes that our high level of exposure to celebrity culture has meant that, just like celebrities, we "construct ourselves into objects that immediately arouse sentiments of desire and approval in others."[8] However, we then fall into a trap that celebrities have been experiencing for years: the split between the public self and the private self.

> Celebrity status always implies a split between a private self
> and a public self. . . . The public presentation of self is always
> a staged activity, in which the human actor presents a "front"
> or "face" to others while keeping a significant portion of the

self in reserve. For the celebrity, the split between the I and the Me is often disturbing. So much so, that celebrities frequently complain of identity confusion.[9]

This split between the public and the private self creates a situation in which we, like the star, find a cognitive dissonance between our two selves. We find ourselves asking, Which self is really me? What if I get found out and people see the real me? We suffer from identity confusion and feel the anxiety that is so pervasive in modern life. We may not all be stars, but we all feel the stars' tension between the public and the private self to an extent. Frankly, living with both selves can be exhausting.

MEDIA ME

The proliferation of media technologies in our culture has changed how we act. Just look at the growing trend of "popping." Teenagers will beat, bully, or humiliate others while filming the incident, and often the crime will be posted on the Internet. One psychologist, commenting on this disturbing trend, noted that it was the presence of a camera that made the young people feel they could engage in such brutal acts with no thought for the victim or the consequence. In our culture today, once a camera is turned on, everything changes. Almost subconsciously we begin to act differently.

My father recently had some old family movies that were filmed in the mid-1960s transferred onto DVD. As I watched, I saw my relatives at a party, nothing really that special—until I noticed that they didn't react to the camera at all. It was as if the camera wasn't there. They seemed totally unconscious of the fact that they were being filmed. Fast-forward to today. Inject a camera into a social situation and everyone begins to act, and before you know it, the video is uploaded to the Internet and being watched by a guy you went to school with, who now lives in the United Arab Emirates.

WE ARE ALL MODELS NOW

Not too long ago, I was catching a plane to a speaking engagement. Joining me on the trip was our state's championship girls' high school basketball team. When the public announcement informed us that our flight would be delayed by an hour, the girls all groaned. But then they reached for their digital cameras and proceeded to spend the next hour photographing each other. This wasn't too unusual, but what caught my attention was the way the camera changed their behavior. Gone were the teenagers excited about traveling. The girls' countenance changed almost instantly as they snapped photos, holding their cameras above eye level in a shot known by seemingly all teenage girls today and seen on millions of their social networking Web site profiles. This photographic trick was first developed by photographers for "girlie" magazines in the 1950s. When women are trying to seduce men, they look up at them with their heads slightly pointed down. This pose is a powerful visual cue that makes men feel a sense of dominance over women and a desire to protect them.

But this wasn't the only pose the girls were using. They were playing with their hair, slightly turning their faces, pouting their lips, leaning forward—all strong visual cues suggesting sexual availability. They were trying out all of these poses in front of their coach, teachers, and parents. I'm sure the girls weren't aware of the messages they were giving off; likely the pictures were more for themselves and their girlfriends than for guys. They were simply acting out a media script that told them how to behave in order to create an identity. These girls, like millions of others around the world, are exposed to a message that furnishes their lives like media wallpaper. This message tells them that social currency and success come from imitating a set of visual cues and creating a mask of sexiness. Sexiness is just one of the many media masks confronting us and acting as a substitute for true character. We have arrived at a time in history when the whole of life has become a stage. The distinction between the stage and the audience has broken down; we have all become players in the media game. We both consume media and act it out. It has become our primary source of identity.

MOVIES, THE NEW BIBLE

When the attacks on the World Trade Center on September 11, 2001, occurred, person after person said to me how much the television footage looked like a movie. People now constantly compare daily events to moments in their media memory—scenes from movies, television, and popular culture.

I once saw a documentary about tribal people living in the Papua New Guinean highlands. They had no written component to their language, yet by heart they could recite up to twenty-five thousand relatives, both living and dead. This seemed amazing to me. But then I thought that, while I couldn't list that many relatives, I almost definitely could remember twenty-five thousand advertising jingles or the basic plots of thousands of television shows and movies. Or I could at least recognize the faces, if not names, of thousands of movie stars, musicians, celebrities, and pro athletes. Indeed, people today compare their successes, looks, and situations with those of movie stars, who, because of their sheer exposure, seem like close friends. The line between celebrity life and our lives is extremely fine; we have trouble discerning where the world of entertainment ends and real life begins. The places to which people in the past looked for guidance in finding identity—such as the church, tradition, and social conventions—have been superseded. People now look to the media for guidance in discovering a sense of self. Therefore, it is no shock that we find people living life as actors. This change in how we see ourselves and how we behave is having a dramatic effect not only on our culture, but also on ourselves.

MEDIA FEEDBACK LOOPS

The stories of the Bible and the history of the people of God seem a million miles away from the reality of our lives because we live in the media landscape. It's a terrain constructed out of the messages we receive most of our waking lives from the millions of movies, television shows, novels, and tidbits of celebrity gossip that we have consumed. They are the stories of our lives, and they provide us with the template from which to borrow, steal, and sculpt new identities. They are the myths from which we learn to act.

Let me explain. The world was shocked by the videotaped beheading of the American reporter Daniel Pearl in Pakistan. This form of media terrorism was adopted in Iraq and Saudi Arabia by al-Qaeda and its affiliates. Several well-publicized hostage cases have ended with the captives being beheaded and the footage of the executions being broadcast over the Internet. Not long after these incidents occurred, a trend began online. Teenage boys from all over the world began posting videos online in which they reenacted these beheadings. Literally hundreds, if not thousands, of videos were posted in which these grisly events were reconstructed. Media analysts and adolescent psychologists began to speculate that what the teenage boys were doing was reenacting the events as a way of processing them, as a way of working through the traumatic media images they had seen. Put simply, they were acting out what they had seen on the screen.

Media theorist Douglas Rushkoff calls this a "media loop": we are influenced by the media we watch and consume, so we start to act ourselves and turn our lives into media events.[10]

In my neighborhood the latest migrant group to arrive have been refugees from Sudan. Our church has been involved in various programs helping them settle into the Australian community. I have been fascinated to observe how Sudanese young people integrate. When I go out, I'll often see teenage Sudanese boys newly arrived from Africa. They aren't too concerned with fashion, and they seem to enjoy riding their bicycles around the streets at high speed, with giant grins on their faces. However, after about six months of living in Australia, things begin to change—starting with their clothes. Gone are the traditional clothes they wore in Africa; these are replaced by baggy jeans, baseball caps, NFL football jerseys, and cornrow hairstyles. When taking a photo of these young Sudanese men, you will often find them flashing U.S.-style gang hand signals. Now, these young men are not even in gangs. In fact, most of them are teetotaling and studious churchgoers. But they are acting out a media script. They come to Australia and find themselves in a contemporary, Western, predominantly white culture that is extremely similar to that of the United States, and so they imitate the most pervasive media identity that they see of Africans, which is hip-hop culture. This is just one more example of the way in which, in our media-drenched culture, we begin to imitate what we see on the screen.

This imitation doesn't only happen in unusual cases like the ones I've just related. Thousands, if not millions, of young women all over the world look to the show *Sex and the City* as a guide to life, even after its finale. You might hear them speak of how they love the show because it reflects the reality of their lives, but the show also shapes their actions. Again, this is the media feedback loop at work.

The same chicken-or-egg question is asked of both sex and violence in the media. Is there more sexual content in the media because we are more sexually aware, or are we in a more sexual age because there is more sexual content in the media? Are violent computer games responsible for more teen violence, or are computer game makers just reflecting the violent reality of the world that teens live in? Both feed off each other: our media reflects our culture, but it also shapes our culture and us. We have grown up in front of screens and cameras; we know what it is to consume media and to perform, even if it is just to those around us. Life has become a media performance, and we already know the lines.

FAITH, THE HORIZONTAL SELF, AND THE LIFE MOVIE

The British explorer and soldier Colonel Francis Younghusband had reason to be worried as he led his troops into the Tibetan city of Lhasa in the winter of 1904.[11] His men had only recently been involved in a skirmish in which 628 local, lightly armed Tibetan horsemen had been killed by machine-gun fire. However, to Younghusband's great surprise, instead of responding in anger over their countrymen's massacre, the inhabitants of Lhasa greeted the British with cheers and applause. Pleasantly surprised, the British politely took off their hats and thanked the Tibetans for their welcome. Unbeknownst to Younghusband and his men, in Tibetan culture people cheered to bring rain down upon unwanted guests, and they clapped in order to repel intruders. This was not a welcome; it was a local show of anger, disgust, and defiance that was lost in translation.

I thought of this story recently as I visited a friend's church. The minister was giving a pep talk to the congregation. He told them that their community was filled with people who were searching for spiritual truth. He admonished them to connect with these people and invite them to come on Sunday. I found myself wondering whether the people in this church's community really were seeking spiritual truth, and if so, were they seeking it in the way the minister imagined? Ironically, on my drive to the service that morning, I had found myself waiting at a red light to turn in to the church parking lot. A car had zipped in front of me, and as I glanced at the young driver, I thought to myself that he was probably, like me, late to the service. When the light changed, however, he kept driving; he didn't turn in to the church. Just then I noticed a large yellow bumper sticker on his car that read "Happy Heathen." *So much for the local neighborhood yearning for spiritual truth*, I thought to myself. Like Colonel Younghusband, we find ourselves getting lost in translation. Ministers and church leaders assume that they are speaking to people who have a vertical sense of self, but those they minister to both inside and outside the church (if they're younger than sixty years old) almost certainly have a horizontal sense of self. People in the church's neighborhood probably were looking for spiritual truth, but in a completely different way than what we are used to. They are looking for truth, meaning, and a sense of self horizontally, not vertically. In fact, most of us probably hold a horizontal sense of self and are not even aware of it.

The emergence of the horizontal self is one of the most pressing challenges for the church in our day. Most of our theology was written by people who lived during the time of the vertical self. Most of our evangelistic approaches were designed to communicate the gospel to people with a vertical sense of self. The same applies to our frameworks of spiritual growth and discipleship. This is why so many Christians, particularly young adults, find such a gulf between their faith and their lives—so much of the teaching that occurs today is based on the assumption that those listening and learning are operating within a framework of the vertical self.

MOVIES AND OUR UNDERSTANDING OF FAITH

A respected pastor and I were having a conversation. Because I'm involved with young adult ministry, she asked me about her son. She was worried about his connection to his faith. She told me she couldn't understand how someone who'd had such profound encounters with the Holy Spirit could seem to be walking away from his faith. I told her not to overestimate the ability of young adults today to simply consume and then discard experiences without allowing them to have any effect on their view of the world whatsoever. She seemed genuinely dumbstruck by my response. But think about it. Teenagers watch a horror film at a sleepover to enjoy the fear and suspense of murder without the carnage and cost. A couple rents a steamy DVD featuring an adulterous affair to feel titillated without the emotional cost of actual relationship breakdown. A group of guys watches a heavyweight bout to enjoy the thrill of physical combat without the risk of injury or personal cost. The entertainment age and the horizontal self have led us to divorce what we believe from what we experience, see, and feel. The elephant in the living room of contemporary Christianity is people's ability to simply sit in church, to consume the experience the way one would a great sporting event, a thrilling movie, or an exciting theme park ride, and then to dispose of it, totally unchanged at the soul level, as they leave the sanctuary. Sure, they might feel challenged, encouraged, or even moved, but the horizontal self simply "feels" the experience and moves on. Don't get me wrong: this can happen anywhere—in traditional churches, emerging churches, and contemporary churches.

FAITH IN THE AGE OF THE HORIZONTAL SELF

Worship service becomes pseudo media event
Church building becomes theme park
Christian leader becomes Christian celebrity
Teaching becomes entertainment
Salvation becomes self-help
Discipleship becomes lifestyle enhancement
Soul becomes self
Denomination becomes brands
Gospel becomes slogan

I am not proposing that we shouldn't engage people with the mediums and media of the day; however, we cannot do so without remembering the great media theorist Marshall McLuhan's adage that the medium is the message. In the entertainment age, we cannot naively think that because we have gathered a crowd, we are necessarily transforming people's lives. I will never forget watching a particular large young-adult worship service. The worship leader was a young man in his twenties. He wore the obligatory rock star uniform: tight black jeans, 1970s Keith Richards hair, stubble, and faux retro T-shirt cut at just the right angle to reveal his well-toned biceps. He barely looked at the crowd of worshippers in front of him, caught up as he was in his emotive, almost pained singing. I couldn't help but notice that many of the young female worshippers in the crowd were staring at him. Afterward, one of my friends told me she couldn't believe how hot the worship leader was.

Now, I have no doubt that the guy was genuine in his worship and that he was unaware of the effect he was having on his audi ence. But without realizing it, he was engaged in acting out the "cool" role. His clothes, his stance, his worshipful concentration, and his guitar were all pulled from a vat of fifty years of media images of rock stars. These images hinted at celebrity, intriguing aloofness, passionate abandon, eroticism, and social power. They were social cues that the girls in the congregation simply could not resist. Without meaning to, he was acting out the social self of "rock-star sexiness" to perfection.

When we use the tools, symbols, and mediums of the entertainment culture, they do not come "value free." We can make our churches cooler, our ministries hipper, our services more entertaining, and our media more cutting edge. Yet we must remember that if we don't take seriously the current crisis of self, if we don't begin to examine how we can reach out to and disciple the horizontal self, our decline will continue. We will move from being communicators of the gospel to acting as communicators of just another lifestyle choice. Christianity becomes just another social self to put on and take off—like a pair of jeans. We, as the church, will find ourselves in the same predicament as those with the worldview of the horizontal self—focused on the external and the temporal, engrossed with sensation, obsessed with refining our image—all the while forgetting that we are created in the image of the Creator.

CHAPTER 5

Pop-Culture Memories
of Wholeness

The movie *Memento* features a character who loses his memory because of a massive head trauma. All that he can recall is short, unconnected shards of memory. Flashes of images and feelings make no sense because of his lack of memory; he is unable to arrange them into a narrative that would explain his past. In many ways this predicament is similar to our culture today. When it comes to the influence of the Christian faith, a great forgetting has occurred. The average citizen of the West is almost totally unaware of the extent to which Christianity has shaped his or her worldview. So many have forgotten the ways in which the biblical imagination has shaped our arts; our concepts of justice, equality, and human rights; our ideas of personhood, of goodness, and morality. So much of what we value as a culture is born out of Christianity; yet average people are unaware of the mountain upon which they stand. This could not be more true of our concepts of identity. Our great forgetting means that we still seek out echoes of eternity when it comes to establishing our identities. But because of our failure to understand our biblical foundations, we grasp and grab at dislocated concepts of self.

DNA RESIDUE OF OUR TRUE SELVES

Just think of all the movies you have watched. Think of the way the woman screams when she is confronted by the killer in the horror movie. Think of the way the hero who has just won a million dollars acts. Think of the villains. Think of the hardened cop who bends the rules to bring crooks to justice. Recall the way the seductress dances, the way the devilishly hip criminal delivers his lines, the way the class goofball falls off his chair, the way the quarterback celebrates his touchdown. All of these memories provide a sort of storehouse of instructions for how to act. With no set identity given to us anymore, we delve into that storehouse to know which way to act, which way to be, which identities or roles to perform. Our culture offers us disposable identities—for example, the sexy identity, the cool identity, the glam identity. Yet when we look behind these identities, we find elements that point us back to a true sense of self. Listen closely enough, and you will hear echoes of wholeness, forgotten shadows of our true selves.

David LaChapelle's documentary *Rise* explores the hip-hop dance cultures of clowning and krumping, which developed in South Central Los Angeles after the LA riots. The movement was an attempt to create a positive alternative for young people to the culture of gangs and drug selling. The dance styles also provided frustrated urban youth with an artistic avenue to physically and creatively express their negative feelings in a positive way. The documentary is a moving depiction of the way music, art, and faith can collide in the unlikeliest of places to bring life. In one part of the film, the dance moves of the young African-American dancers are spliced with images of traditional African tribal dancing. The similarities are so uncanny that LaChapelle simply assumed that the young people whose dancing he was documenting had copied moves they had seen in old documentaries of African tribal dancing. But LaChapelle discovered he was wrong. Before the movie was released, he organized a showing of the film as thanks to all of the young people who had aided in its production. When the scene of the African dancing came on, the crowd was shocked. They began to cheer and pump their fists. Growing up in South Central and Watts, they had never been exposed to images of traditional African dancing. When they realized the dancing style they had created was uncannily similar to that of their ancestors, they were deeply moved. It was as if some cultural DNA had been passed down to them. A connection was established with their roots, and they found that a part of Africa's culture was still inside of them.

The same dynamic occurs when we look at some of the social masks that people act out, such as sexy, cool, or glam. On one hand, these social selves take us away from our true selves. They move us toward parody and the perversion of our humanity. Yet when we dig deep enough behind the clichés and performances, we find tiny grains of truth, memories of wholeness. To move forward effectively toward our true selves in our culture today, we must examine these social selves and their power to influence our behavior both negatively and positively. Let's examine some of the identities commonly acted out in youth and young (and not-so-young) adult culture.

CHAPTER 6

The Social Self of Sexy

The screech of the car's tires announced their arrival in the gas station parking lot. Their purple sports car bore a Playboy bunny sticker and pumped out R&B bass lines. They both disembarked from the vehicle as if they were arriving at an awards show. They were in their midtwenties and wore the classic contemporary uniform: miniskirts, tight-fitting tank tops, dyed blonde hair, perfect tans, and extensive makeup. Their physiques gave away the fact that these girls spent a lot of time toning up at the gym. As they filled their gas tank, they tried to act casual, but it was obvious that they were anxious to know if they had an audience. Unfortunately, I was the only one in the parking lot, and as they walked inside to pay, they both glanced at me with their best seductive looks. Wow.

You are probably wondering if this scene was enough to send me running to my accountability group. My honest answer is no. As the young women drove away, I realized they were acting out a learned script. Beneath the makeup and grooming, beneath the diligently learned visual cues of seduction, it was obvious that these two girls were actually deeply insecure. They were not at all interested in me; I was simply playing a key function in their performance. I was their audience. They wanted to be noticed. They wanted me—a man—to ogle them, to affirm that their carefully orchestrated act of "sexiness" made them people of worth. They wanted to know that the public "self" they had created had been a success. It probably wouldn't have mattered if I were female; I'm sure they would have been just as happy to be the recipients of female envy as of male appreciation. Both would have confirmed their social currency—the sense that they were worthwhile human beings. Both would have aided them in their misguided attempts to find their true selves.

SEXY IS EVERYWHERE

Our culture is obsessed with the idea of sexiness. It is ubiquitous. We cannot walk down the street without seeing advertisements featuring models both male and female in various sexy poses. Entertainment magazines each year announce the sexiest people in our culture. Music videos that would have been classified as soft porn only a few years ago now play around the clock on music video channels aimed at young teenagers. It is almost obligatory for any young actress or female musician or sports star to appear in a sexy photo shoot in a men's magazine. Weekly women's magazines promise tips on how to be sexier. You can even exercise in pole dancing and stripping classes at your local gym.

Sexiness seems to transcend age, as actors in their sixties are dubbed "sexy" by the press. Even young children are no longer immune from the trend. An elementary teacher friend of mine told me of a recent school dance where seven-year-old girls danced in incredibly sexual styles, mimicking what they had seen in music videos. You can buy dolls wearing miniskirts with garter belts underneath. We are a culture obsessed with sexy. It is one of the most dominant disposable identities we encounter. It has become one of the chief acts of the horizontal self.

SEXY BOMBS

Now, you could simply explain away this whole phenomenon by saying that we as a culture are naturally obsessed with the concept of sexiness because we are a culture obsessed with sex. Although that may seem to be the obvious answer, I believe we need to scratch under the surface to discover whether something else is going on.

When I was growing up, if someone used the word *sexy*, he or she was almost always describing a person who was sexually appealing. But things have changed. At first we started hearing the word *sexy* attached to women's shoes or to fashion, but then it moved on to cars, shopping sprees, computers, and apartments. Then things started getting really strange: *sexy* began to describe things that were definitely not sexy in the traditional use of the word. I read about sexy football plays, sexy economic policies, sexy art galleries. But it became truly bizarre when a U.S. military general described a bombing raid on the Taliban in Afghanistan as "sexy stuff," and former British prime minister Tony Blair was quoted as saying an intelligence report needed to be "sexed up." All of a sudden the most boring parts of our culture needed to be made sexy—anything from rainfall totals to science to accounting. Obviously something was going on, but things hit home for me when a pastor friend told me his ministry needed to be sexier!

The word *sexy* is now a cultural phenomenon that means so much more than sexual attraction. *Sexy* means a variety of things, and to label something as sexy is to overlay a number of meanings on it. Cultural critic Ariel Levy wrote, "For something to be noteworthy it must be 'sexy.' Sexiness is no longer just about being arousing or alluring, it's about being worthwhile."[1] Banks, herb gardens, and universities can all wear the public mask of "sexiness." It is the perfect outerwear in the age of the horizontal self.

DESIRE

To label something sexy is to say that it is desirable. The executive who describes the cell phone he covets as sexy is placing a value of desirability upon that item. When the supermodel is described as the world's sexiest woman, she is being touted as a woman whom most men would desire to be with. The pastor who told me he wants to make his ministry sexier is really just saying he wants to make it more desirable to people so they'll get involved.

When people in our culture attempt to act out being sexy, they are really just trying to act in a way that makes them desirable to others—not necessarily as a sexual partner, but often just as a person others find interesting and valuable. For those with a horizontal view of self, being desired, being the object of intrigue and the center of attention, is like winning the Super Bowl.

PLEASURE

The cultural concept of sexiness is connected to pleasure. The person who is sexy is someone who provides pleasure. Individuals who are given the social label of sexy are people who both provide pleasure to others and love experiencing pleasure themselves. Consider the cinema sex kittens of the 1960s: they directly contrasted with their "uptight" mothers. They created situations in which pleasure was exercised.

Today, in the age of the horizontal self, in which delayed gratification is downplayed and temporary pleasure is valued, the media mask of "pleasure provider" carries enormous cultural currency.

POWER

Sexiness carries strong connotations of power. For many men, sexiness accompanies their cultural power, but sexiness has become a culturally acceptable means of exercising social power for women as well. This power can be exercised to gain control over men, but it can also be exercised against other women.

Brigitte Bardot, the French film star, pioneered the media mask of sexiness that we see everywhere today. Bardot was a new kind of woman. In contrast to the tightly curled and coiffed hairstyles of the classic female beauties of her time, her long, lush, tousled hair was described as "bedroom hair." One commentator at the time wrote that Bardot's hair made her look as if she had just gotten out of bed after making love. While older film stars, such as Jayne Mansfield, Betty Grable, and Rita Hayworth, were obviously groomed by their movie houses to appeal to male audiences with a carefully rehearsed performance, Bardot seemed to be sexy because she wanted to be. On-screen her "sexy" public face seemed to be a message to the world rather than just a play to men. It was as much a challenge to women as it was an appeal to men. As movie historian Sean French wrote, "She embodied—all too visibly—a youthful sexual arrogance, an arrogance that was all the more shocking for being justified. If anything, her affronting self-assertion was addressed more to women than to men: I can have any man I want, she seemed to say, and any other qualities, all your qualities—intelligence, charm, humor, ties of affection or duty—are useless."[2]

Bardot became the symbol of a new kind of female public self.

Her whole life seemed to be defined by her sexiness. She was often photographed at the exclusive French seaside of St. Tropez in a shocking new swimming costume known as the bikini. She also symbolized the 1960s sexual revolution. She was open about her appetite for sun, sex, and pleasure. When she first appeared on the scene, Bardot caused a sensation with her public self of sexiness, but the public self she pioneered is now ubiquitous among young and not-so-young women. It is a public self that uses sexiness as power, as a way of gaining social status and meaning in the age of the horizontal self.

Many young women today have grown up with the post-feminist phenomenon of "girl power" as exemplified by groups such as the Spice Girls. Instead of being passive sexual objects, girls are encouraged to use their sexuality and femininity to their advantage. Just listen to the popular music marketed toward young women today: song after song reaffirms the message that young women's sexuality is the pathway to their social success. The woman who has mastered the Sexy social self wields tremendous social power in our culture today. Sociologists have termed this phenomenon *performative sexuality*, noting that often this very public display of sexual power is completely disconnected from one's personal sex life. What is important is not what is going on in someone's real life but the show she is putting on for the audience of her peers.

GOOD-BYE, NORMA JEAN

Brigitte Bardot was not alone in fostering the modern concept of the Sexy social self; it also began with Marilyn Monroe. The famous image of her standing over a subway grating, the wind from the train below causing her skirt to billow up, has helped define the modern media image of sexiness.

Marilyn was born Norma Jeane Mortenson and baptized Norma Jeane Baker. Because her mother was too sick to care for her, she spent much of her childhood moving from foster home to foster home. Living in Los Angeles, she grew up in the shadow of Hollywood, and the lure of the silver screen and fame became the only ray of hope in her otherwise poor and dismal childhood. Her road toward fame began when she started hanging around Hollywood parties. This led to modeling and then acting in films. Marilyn realized early on that her sexuality could be a powerful weapon in a world in which she felt powerless. She carefully cultivated a public persona that became the prototype of sexiness that we see so often in popular culture. She changed her hair from brunette to blonde; she changed her name from Norma Jeane to Marilyn. She changed how she walked, creating her famous hip-swaying waddle, which—although relatively tame compared to what we are exposed to today—caused a social sensation in the 1950s. When she picked dresses for public events, she made sure she pushed the envelope of acceptable decency. She even invented the personality that we label today as the "dumb blonde."

Marilyn, contrary to what the public saw, was a complicated and intelligent woman. She created a pop-culture icon, a public persona that became a sex symbol that still defines our culture over half a century later. Yet the sad legacy of her life was that despite all the attention she garnered, despite her fame, she could never find happiness. Her biographer, Barbara Leaming, wrote, "Against almost impossible personal and professional odds, she had created something brilliant and magical—'Marilyn Monroe.' Her creation had brought immense pleasure to millions of people, and would continue to do so long after she was gone. The world loved Marilyn. Yet in the end she felt utterly unloved and alone."[3]

Monroe's public performance of the Sexy social self gave her fame. It led her to wealth. It enabled her to seduce some of the most powerful men of her time. Yet it was external. On the inside she was still the girl pushed from foster home to foster home, desperately trying to be liked. Behind so much of her act of sexuality was an attempt to connect with a father figure, to be loved as she was, not as she was seen. However, the battle between these two selves—the public and the private—was intense. At age thirty-six, the woman who will always be remembered as the archetypal modern sex symbol died alone. There is almost a tragic poetry in the fact that when she was found dead on her bed by her housekeeper, her hand was holding the telephone receiver. The woman whom the whole world wanted, who had created the public persona par excellence, could not connect in time with the outside world. In her darkest time of need, she had no one to call.

CHAPTER 7

The Social Self of Cool

My brother Glen is into music. He collects vinyl and is constantly trawling the Internet for some new sound. He will often turn up at my house with a new artist or band I "must hear." It could be anything from Korean hip-hop to experimental German punk to some obscure early '80s funk. One day he arrived with a clutch of records by the '70s jazz rock band Steely Dan.

"Not the band who wrote 'Reelin' in the Years'!" I told him. The tune is played ad nauseam on bad FM stations the world over. He said to push past that song and listen to the band, which he said represented to perfection the subgenre of what some jokingly refer to as "yacht rock." We both became hooked, so when we heard that the band had reunited and was going to play a gig in our town, we knew we had to go. It was the first time I had been to a retro concert, and the first thing that shocked me was how young my brother and I were compared to the rest of the concertgoers, who must have had an average age of fifty-five.

The audience seemed to be divided into two types of baby boomers: cool, stylish, older architect types dressed in black suits with black T-shirts, and aging hippies with much-cherished and long-held ponytails. As I looked around, I realized something strange was going on here—a bunch of people my parents' age had shown up at a rock concert. Being a recent convert to the music, I was there to enjoy the show. But for the baby boomers around me, the concert was a way to relive teenage memories. It was as if they were trying to resurrect their former youth identities through the music. An almost palpable sense of loss hung in the air as memories came flooding back.

The rock concert was a giant reminder of what it was to be young and hip in the '70s, but it was also a testament to the power of "cool" in our society. For over half a century, the cultural force of coolness has deeply informed how we see ourselves and, through movies, media, and music, has given millions a template from which to construct their identities.

In many ways *cool* is the kissing cousin of *sexy*. It is in some ways the male equivalent of sexy. Sure, I know guys can be sexy and girls can be cool, but you'll hear *sexy* more often attached to females and *cool* to males. Like *sexy*, *cool* is just as mysterious and hard to pin down. Perhaps even more than *sexy*, *cool* is used to describe an inordinate number of situations, objects, people, and activities. Never before has a word been so often used but so hard to define. Most of us use this word on a daily basis—we try to be cool, yet we cannot define this slippery adjective.

Today the idea of cool is almost universal. It powers the global youth economy. Cultural critics Dick Pountain and David Robins wrote, "Cool is destined to become the dominant ethic among the younger generations of the whole developed world and billions of 'wannabes' in developing countries."[1] A vast reservoir of media images fuels our understanding of cool. It is a tradition of cool that stretches from the early blues and jazz musicians, to the tough-guy detectives of film noir, to the hard-drinking and hard-living novelists of the Beat generation, to teen rebel movie stars, to the rock stars and the avant-garde conceptual artists, to punk rock pioneers, to the hard-as-nails cinema cowboys of Westerns, to gangsta rappers. This history of cool carries incredibly potent social power for anyone who can harness it. Thus, it is no surprise that cool is used by almost everyone today, from corporations that encourage youths to make "rebellious purchases," to political candidates who are photographed with rock stars to gain polling points, to Iraqi Shiite insurgents who use jihadist hip-hop to encourage young men to become suicide bombers.

Cool has become one of the dominant ways people act out a public self. Pountain and Robins explain:

> Cool is not just some "phase you go through," something that you "grow out of," but rather something that if once attained remains for life. . . . This attitude is in the process of becoming the dominant type of relation between people in Western societies, a new secular virtue. No-one wants to be good any more, they want to be Cool, and this desire is no longer just confined to teenagers but is to be found in a sizeable minority even of the over-50's.[2]

For males in our culture who can manage to perfect the Cool social self, sexiness is almost always a by-product. And just as our culture promises those who master the Sexy social self a meaningful and fulfilling life, the same is promised to those who can master the Cool persona.

AFRICA AND COOL

The story of cool begins in a very different place than we might imagine. Three of the most common cool expressions—"That's hip," "I dig that," and "That's cool"—have their origins in African tribal culture, specifically in the Yoruba and Ibo cultures of West Africa. Male warriors would hold themselves in a way that they would describe as "cool," that is, calm and controlled. The concept was also linked to true understanding, to a view of the world as it really was. Dick Pountain and David Robins write, "*Cool*, or *itutu* contained meanings of conciliation and gentleness of character, the ability to defuse fights and disputes, of generosity and grace."[3]

The interchangeable concepts of "cool" and "hip" were brought to the United States by African slaves who found themselves exercising it as a way of dealing with the situation they found themselves in as slaves. This mask endured from the plantation into modern urban America. The idea of cool for African-Americans became a way of carrying oneself with dignity and a way of understanding oneself. But it was also a defense mechanism. Pountain and Robins continue:

> Once transported to America, Africans were forced to surrender their physical integrity and work as plantation slaves, but perhaps they felt that they could protect some part of their spiritual integrity by clinging to Cool, which afforded them a symbolic territory beyond the jurisdiction of their white owners. . . . All that their white owners were allowed to see were caricatures of subservience, heavy with irony, behind Cool masks that concealed the contempt and rage that the slaves felt, the frank expression of which would have brought down harsh physical punishment.[4]

By acting cool, one was able to negotiate a life threatened by the constant potential of violence. As cultural essayist Daniel Harris observes, "Coolness is an aesthetic of the streets . . . specifically designed to alert potential predators that one is impregnable to assault. . . . Coolness grows out of a sense of threat of living in metropolitan war zones."[5] However, cool moved beyond just the African-American community. As migrants collided with one another in places such as New York City, acting cool became a way that people from various histories, cultures, and countries could reinvent themselves in a new country and survive in a new urban landscape.

WHAT COOL IS ALL ABOUT

With the right clothes, the right jazz records, the right friends, and of course the right attitude, the migrant son of tailors from a small Polish village could reinvent himself as an American big-city hipster. Jazz contributed greatly to this process as the first modern popular music to spread the idea of cool beyond urban centers into small-town America. The first real explosion of cool into the public's consciousness can be traced back to Norman Mailer's 1957 article "The White Negro: Superficial Reflections on the Hipster," published in Harper's *Bazaar* magazine. Mailer described the dilemma facing young people of the mid-twentieth century, who lived in a culture that promised them a suburban paradise only to deliver the Holocaust, the constant threat of nuclear war, and a bleak and soulless materialism. Mailer loudly proclaimed that the only answer for young people was to become "hip." Commenting on Mailer's essay, cultural critic Thomas Frank wrote:

> "The only life-giving answer" to the deathly drag of American civilization, Mailer wrote, was to tear oneself from the security of physical and spiritual certainty, to live for immediate pleasures rather than the postponement of gratification associated with the "work ethic," "to divorce oneself from society, to exist without roots, to set out on that uncharted journey with the rebellious imperatives of the self."[6]

I took a break from writing this chapter to make a trip to my local donut store for a milk shake. As I returned to my car, I walked past a small huddle of teenagers hanging around outside the store. They were dressed in black, each wearing a T-shirt bearing the name of a heavy metal band and sporting baseball caps with images of marijuana leaves on them. They gave me their most intimidating stares as I passed them. But I smiled to myself as I drove away, thinking of how their entire way of behavior has been influenced by a writer they will never hear of, who wrote an article they will never read, yet that article has set the tone for their whole public image. Mailer largely borrowed his ideas from the Beat writers and poets, such as Jack Kerouac, Allen Ginsberg, and William S. Burroughs. They, in turn, borrowed a lot of their ideas of cool from African-Americans, particularly the bop jazz musicians they hung out with. The Beat writers saw that the answer to society's problems was to learn from those on the margins of American culture. They lived among and copied the lifestyles of small-time criminals, the mentally ill, bohemians, and homosexuals. But Mailer felt the answer lay primarily in imitating the life and spirit of African-Americans. For some time white American artists and thinkers had admired African-American culture, which they had discovered through the jazz subculture. Mailer wrote that the key to resisting the dominant modernist culture was to learn from the African-American ideas of hip and cool. To be cool was to live on the edge of culture—to reject it by living in its shadows, avoiding convention and conformity. Instead of living out the narrow life-script offered by society, Mailer believed that by being cool, humans could reembrace a deep, primal need for quest and adventure. Many responded to Mailer's rallying call, and the beatnik movement began, permanently etching the idea of cool into the public's mind.

As cool moved beyond those who understood its original

ethos, it began to change. No longer was it simply a tool of dignity and survival; it became a way of defining yourself as an adolescent growing up in the midst of modern social alienation. It didn't take long for marketers to realize how much money could be made from exploiting young people's desire to find identity through cool. Cool was now a fad that began to sweep the world, starting with the generation of teenagers born after the war. No longer was cool an identification with the poor; rather, it became an attempt to steal some of the perceived street cred of the poor for personal gain. In a culture in which media and marketing had made personal image paramount, cool was a way of impressing others. As soon as cool hit the public imagination, this corruption of its original mode occurred. Writing in 1957, hip pioneer and author Jack Kerouac noted how cool had changed:

> To think that I had so much to do with it . . . and I was already sick of the whole subject. Nothing can be more dreary than "coolness" . . . postured, actually secretly rigid coolness that covers up the fact that the character is unable to convey anything of force or interest, a kind of sociological coolness soon to become a fad up into the mass of middleclass youth. . . . All this was about to sprout out all over America even down to high school level and be attributed in part to my doing![7]

Cool became a way of being seen. It moved from an attitude to an aesthetic. Hollywood, rock 'n' roll, and a booming consumer market ensured that cool became the perfect social mask to wear in an age in which media was beginning to dominate social consciousness. This version of cool is exactly the same as sexy; both are all about being watched. As people became less defined by their contribution to society and by their pasts, the new media landscape was all about producing the right image. Cool was a performance. As pop culture historian John Leland notes, cool "requires an audience. . . . It exists in public view, its parameters defined by the people watching it."[8]

The performance of cool requires an ever-evolving knowledge of the right information. Someone who wishes to be cool must know the right clothes to wear, the right music to listen to, the right places to be seen, the right products and technologies to use, and the right attitude to portray. To miscalculate one of these factors even slightly can mean that one is no longer judged cool by one's peers. Thus, the person attempting to be cool faces tremendous pressure to remain relevant. Cool can bring social acceptance and status, but it can also leave you with the giant burden of constantly remaining in touch with the changing landscape of what is cool and what is not. Because we are so used to seeing the public performance, we no longer question it. Yet a closer examination of cool reveals fascinating insights into who we wish to be.

COOL IS A SEARCH FOR OUR TRUE SELVES

Consider the clothes we buy. The other day I needed a new jacket. I went to my local department store's men's department. The clothes for sale said a lot about our desire for authenticity. I saw distressed jeans that had been treated and washed in factories to make them look like they have a story or a past. Originally, jeans were worn as a way of identifying with the working class, who wore the tough material in factories and on farms. But we now pay top dollar for jeans with the right worn look.

I also saw faded '70s-style T-shirts for sale, featuring logos of burger joints and universities that never existed. There were faded Ramones and Rolling Stones T-shirts, which no doubt would be bought and worn by people who are not fans of the bands—they simply want to capture a sense of vintage rock cool.

And there were bright hooded tops featuring retro '80s designs meant to capture the mystique that many from Generation Y feel about the decade in which they were born.

What was for sale were not just clothes to be worn but opportunities to communicate authenticity and cultural currency. Cool offers middle-class people a chance to escape their self-consciousness and to be comfortable and affluent. The teenager from the leafy green, well-to-do suburb can, with a flick of his cap and a pair of baggy pants, take on the gangster persona in an attempt to have the street cred of the ghetto rub off on him. The performance of cool offers the social actor the benefits of imitating a cultural outsider without any of the social cost. Cool gives those who feel entrapped by the normality and conformity of modern mass culture a chance to escape into a fantasy world of faux danger and false rebellion.

Last week I pulled up next to a customized black SUV at a red light. The car windows were tinted and covered in skate stickers and skulls and crossbones. The driver's tattooed arm leaned out of the window. He looked down at me through his sunglasses, the picture of cool. However, the situation became more comical as I looked into the backseat and saw two little girls no more than four years old looking at coloring books. It was as if this young man felt that his masculinity had been compromised by his role of father to these two little girls, and somehow his Cool persona was supposed to act as a visual signal that he had not been domesticated.

Behind the idea of cool is a deep desire to discover or rediscover personal authenticity. Of course, the performative version of cool that we have now is almost the polar opposite of authenticity; it is about projecting a false self, about creating a surface identity different from one's interior identity.

CHAPTER 8

The Social Self of Glamorous

M y wife has been obsessed with the movie *Breakfast at Tiffany's* since I met her. Filmed in 1961, the movie tells the story of Holly Golightly. The role of Holly was played by Audrey Hepburn and made her an icon of Hollywood glamour and style. She became the first female Hollywood star whose primary appeal was to females rather than males. When Holly experiences "the mean reds," her term for being afraid when you don't know what you are afraid of, she gets up early, dons her most elegant dress and pearls, buys breakfast to go, and window-shops at the famous Tiffany's jewelry store. As the story unfurls, we find that the sophisticated, chic party girl is really a scared, anxious girl named Lulu Mae from a poor family in the South.[1] We discover that she is running from her past; she is simultaneously trying to find herself and running from herself. She attempts to inject meaning and a sense of mystery into her life by pretending to live a life that is glamorous. She loves shopping, or at least window-shopping, at

Tiffany's because it gives her life a sense of the transcendent; it adds a touch of magic to her mundane days.

For people living in the age of the horizontal self, in which the culture has drained everyday life of any sense of the sacred or the spiritual, glamour has become a way that ordinary people try to capture that sense of mystery. Celebrity worship, fashion magazines, and luxury goods all offer people the chance to take on the Glamorous public self. Having culturally lost a sense of the sacred, we grasp at what seems the closest replica of mystery and transcendence. We fall into the trap of worshipping the creation instead of the Creator. As Paul wrote in his letter to the Romans, we have "worshiped and served created things rather than the Creator" (1:25). Idolatry is misguided worship, yet it is still facilitated by a desire to worship. Our embrace of the social selves of Cool, Sexy, and Glamorous reveals our capitulation to the worldview of the horizontal self, but it also reveals a subconscious desire within us to return to the vertical sense of self.

THE PARADOX OF COOL/ SEXY/ GLAM

As I began my research for this book, I asked all kinds of people I encountered and groups to whom I was speaking who they thought was cool or sexy or glamorous. Normally they would reel off a list of celebrities. But then I would press them and ask them about people who they actually knew in person. They then would be able to name friends or acquaintances who they thought were trying to be one of these things. I would then continue to press them and ask them who they thought was genuinely cool. People would struggle. But then occasionally they would name someone whom they thought was genuinely cool. When I asked what made them cool, people would almost always scratch their heads and say, "I guess he does not care what people think about him" or

"He seems to have a confidence or a sense of togetherness about him" or "He just seems so alive." This was what I began to call the "paradox of cool" (or sexy or glam, as the case may be) at work. That is, the more you try to be cool, the less cool you will be. And strangely, often the more you embed your identity in a vertical sense of self, the more people living under a horizontal self will see something in you that will draw them to you.

HE DOES NOT KNOW WHO HE IS

I was speaking at a church service about faith and young adults when I was approached by some young women in their twenties who asked me why there were no eligible guys left in the church (if only I had a dollar . . .). I looked around and spotted a guy who looked the same age as them. He was over six feet tall, well built, and handsome. He stood talking to a friend in a casual stance. He was probably the hippest-dressed guy in the room. I nodded toward him and said to the girls, "What about him? Is he single?"

They rolled their eyes at each other and said, "Yes, he is single— but no way."

I said, "What? Are you kidding me—this guy is single? He looks like a male model!"

One of the girls replied, "Yeah, but he doesn't know who he is."

Despite the fact that he fulfilled all of the requirements for being attractive in our culture, his lack of self-awareness meant that he also lacked that indescribable quality that the term *cool* encompasses.

I remember speaking at a conference for young adults when one of the other speakers took to the podium. His looks wouldn't have stopped traffic if he walked down the street. He was about a million miles away from any culturally approved idea of sexy. But then he began to speak, and everything changed. He spoke passionately about his faith, revealing a deep commitment to his calling of ministry and mission, and he also showed a healthy ability to laugh at himself. As he spoke, the audience was almost silent. I cannot describe it properly, but he possessed an awesome sense of personal power that had nothing to do with aggression or self-advancement. He seemed almost like a warrior from some long-lost army. He most definitely knew who he was.

Most fascinating to me about this speaker was the reaction of the females in the room. They were entranced. It was as if he were drawing something primal out of a deep place inside them. Something indefinable was happening; people were drawn to him like iron to a magnet. The phrase "sexual attraction" is too limiting to describe what was going on—there was a deeper mystery, a spiritual moment at play. I learned that there is also a paradox of sexy as well as a paradox of cool.

Our culture's obsession with the concepts of sexy and cool goes beyond an addiction to sex or consumerism. On one hand, these concepts represent a diminishment of our humanity, an attempt to commodify our God-given identity. Instead of moving us toward our true selves, they move us away from ourselves. On the other hand, both concepts attempt to capture a sense of self that our culture has forgotten. When we encounter someone with a special indefinable quality that we find intriguing, that person elicits a reaction in us that reveals that something else is going on. We use the purest senses of the words *sexy* and *cool* and *glam* to describe this mystery, this unknowability, this transcendence that we occasionally sense in people.

CHAPTER 9

Say Hello to Your Future Self

We must look beneath the surface of the public personas, the media masks, and the false selves. We see a desire for truth, albeit misguided. We know that deep down we desire to connect and be ourselves with people who are whole, people who echo a sense of the eternal. Certain individuals are intriguing to us because they seem to be *alive*. Survey after survey tells us that confidence is the most attractive quality we find in other people. We value a sense of knowing one's self and a sense of mystery that hints at both tranquillity and strength. Fascinatingly, these are the same qualities we attempt to describe when we use the word *cool*, but we find ourselves back at the original African meaning of *cool*: someone who is strong, calm, and at peace; someone who "knows"; someone who is filled with grace and generosity.

We stumble and spit out the words *sexy*, *cool*, and *glam* to describe others because our secular culture has lost the language to describe the deep yearning we all have to return to our true,

God-ordained selves. When we meet someone who exhibits that indescribable sense of mystery, we struggle to integrate the experience within the framework of understanding provided by our culture. It is almost as if we encounter in that person a sense of "rightness," a quality we are drawn to, an echo of wholeness. It is as if that person awakens in us a memory long forgotten. We sense in that person an inaudible call from God's future. The book of Ecclesiastes tells us that God has "set eternity in the human heart; yet no one can fathom what God has done from beginning to end" (3:11).

Maybe when we are drawn to someone who has that indescribable quality, we are drawn to that sense of eternity in them, that hint of holy balance and rightness. Yet as the verse from Ecclesiastes says, we cannot understand the full picture. We cannot see from beginning to end. We fail to realize that these echoes of eternity that we sense in others are calling cards from our future selves.

FUTURE HUMANS

Prodigious savants are people who, usually through some kind of brain trauma, have developed almost superhuman abilities. Some savants are able to memorize thousands upon thousands of books. Others can draw by memory and in incredible detail buildings or landscapes that they have seen days earlier. Some are able to play the most complicated pieces of music after hearing them only once, and others develop mind-boggling mathematical skills.

The number of prodigious savants in the world is small (about one hundred), and thus they are of great interest to the medical and scientific community. Some of these people are born with brain traumas, but others are affected later in life through injury, stroke, or aneurysm. For example, a person may have very little interest or ability in art, but she is in a car accident in which she suffers a brain injury, and almost overnight she is able to paint with extraordinary creativity and skill.

Prodigious savants challenge the traditional understanding of the way humans develop ability and skill, which normally is through practice and education. But what prodigious savants illustrate is that within the human mind exist incredible abilities, although locked and untapped. The scientific explanation behind savants' remarkable abilities has to do with the neurology of the brain and the relationship between its left and right hemispheres. Our culture tends to favor the more rational left brain, and the more creative right brain is suppressed. However, because prodigious savants have suffered a trauma in their left brain, their right brain is unchecked and able to develop in amazing ways. As a person of faith, when I think of these miraculously gifted people, I think of the words of the apostle Paul in 1 Corinthians:

> There are also heavenly bodies and there are earthly bodies; but the splendor of the heavenly bodies is one kind, and the splendor of the earthly bodies is another. The sun has one kind of splendor, the moon another and the stars another; and star differs from star in splendor.
>
> So will it be with the resurrection of the dead. The body that is sown is perishable, it is raised imperishable; it is sown in dishonor, it is raised in glory; it is sown in weakness, it is raised in power; it is sown a natural body, it is raised a spiritual body.
>
> If there is a natural body, there is also a spiritual body. (15:40–44)

Paul is speaking of the future resurrection of believers; he is pointing to the time when those who follow Christ will be raised with their bodies and selves transformed from natural bodies into what Paul describes as "spiritual bodies." I wonder if the amazing creativity, talents, and skills shown by prodigious savants actually lie dormant in every human, and maybe those skills are foretastes of the kind of humans we will be when we, as Paul wrote, are resurrected in glory in our spiritual bodies.

Do we dare to dream what it will be like to be human without the degrading effects of sin, evil, and death? Imagine yourself as you are now, but redeemed—that is, amplified, expanded, improved beyond belief. Paul is talking about *you* minus all of the effects of sin, the Fall, and death. Sit and pause for a minute to meditate on this. In the future you will exist minus all of your current flaws, your fears, your dysfunctions, your jealousy, and your anger. This redeemed you is yourself, but with your positives amplified, your talents expanded, your attributes multiplied, and your maturity fulfilled. It is you exactly as God wished you to be. This is a revolutionary concept when it comes to understanding ourselves. This is the real you.

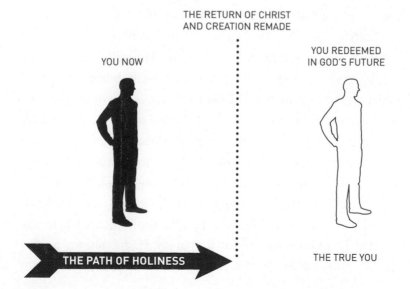

THE RETURN OF CHRIST
AND CREATION REMADE

YOU NOW

YOU REDEEMED
IN GOD'S FUTURE

THE PATH OF HOLINESS

THE TRUE YOU

JESUS' RESURRECTION BODY POINTS
TO THE REAL YOU

If you are at all like me, you have trouble grasping the idea of yourself fully redeemed as God designed you. It's hard to contemplate what you could be like. It just seems so far into the future, so fanciful. All I can imagine are bad science fiction movies. But the people to whom Paul was writing had a definite point of reference from which to understand their future selves: the risen Christ.

Paul begins 1 Corinthians 1 by reminding his readers that they exist within a network of believers, five hundred of whom met with the resurrected Christ and are still living to tell about it. For this community, the doctrine of the resurrection was not some theological abstraction; it was a living, breathing memory that was only a few decades old. Just the other day my parents were telling me the story of my birth. My mother was past my due date, so my parents went for a long walk to try to bring on my birth. For them this memory seems like yesterday, although it was actually thirty-three years ago, almost the same passage of time between the rising of the Messiah and Paul's letter to the Corinthians. So when Paul links the resurrection glory of Christ to the future glory of the believers, his readers understand that he is talking about something akin to a super-self, humanity turned up, improved beyond belief. If we think about Christ in his resurrected form, we get a picture of our future selves. He does things that seem very human—eats breakfast (John 21:12), meets with people (Acts 1:2–4), walks (Luke 24:15)—yet he also does things beyond the ability of humanity as we know it, such as ascending to heaven (Acts 1:9), disappearing (Luke 24:31), and passing through walls (John 20:26). Through his resurrection, Christ has ushered in a new potential for humanity. He has shown us that God's original plans for humanity sketched out in the garden of Eden are now being completed in our time. The resurrected Christ shows us what it is to be fully human. He points us away from our falsely constructed public selves and beckons us toward our souls, our true selves.

SELF OVER SOUL

In our contemporary climate of faith, such an understanding of self as laid out by Paul is almost unheard-of. The ancient art of cultivating this future self, of shaping our souls, is an almost completely forgotten practice among believers today. As people with a horizontal view of self, we spend so much time cultivating our outward appearances and shaping our public performances that we neglect our interior lives. That is to say, we neglect our souls. During the early 1980s, sociologist Robert Bellah and his associates noted a shift in how Americans saw themselves.[1] No longer did they talk much of souls, as their forebears had for centuries. Instead, people used the word *self* to describe themselves. If we are to regain a genuine sense of identity in a culture that has reduced life to acting, we must rediscover what it is to cultivate our souls.

Theologian and writer Eugene Peterson passionately delineates the difference between an understanding of self and of soul:

> In our current culture, "soul" has given way to "self" as the term of choice to designate who and what we are. Self is the soul minus God. Self is what is left of soul with all the transcendence and intimacy squeezed out, the self with little or no reference to God (transcendence) or others (intimacy). . . . Setting the two words side by side triggers a realization that a fundamental aspect of our identity is under assault every day. We live in a culture that has replaced soul with self.[2]

Peterson could not be clearer: our culture has given us only a pale imitation of our identity in the form of the self. We need to revive the practice of cultivating our souls for the well-being of ourselves, our churches, our mission, and our world. To escape the public self with its emphasis on the surface of our personalities, we need to focus on our interior selves. To discover and move toward our true selves, we must put aside our misapprehensions about spiritual growth and dive into the well of holiness.

HOLINESS REIMAGINED

As I was researching for this book, I visited my local library and filled my arms with all kinds of dense sociology books about the contemporary view of self. As I headed for the exit, I decided to pick up some light reading. I grabbed a book entitled *When Box Hill Was a Village* by Gordon Moyes.[3] My only real interest in the book was that it was about the town I live in and in which my church is located, Box Hill, Victoria. The book sat next to my bed, unread for several weeks, as I made a point of diving deep into my research on the contemporary self. But struggling to get to sleep one night, I picked up Moyes's book. It is a collection of Moyes's memories of growing up in my neighborhood during the late 1940s. I had never read a book about my own neighborhood, so it was pleasant reading, a distraction from the heavy research I was doing. But the more I read, the more intrigued I became.

First, I discovered that Moyes was a Christian, and the book spoke of his journey toward faith. Second, Moyes was involved in ministry with the same denomination as I am, in the same part of town, and even on the same streets. These similarities, however, were not what surprised me. I was exhausted, but I was so interested that I read the book from cover to cover. What kept me interested was the sheer world of difference between the sense of self exhibited by the people in Moyes's book and my reality of doing ministry in the same locations sixty years later with young adults whose understanding of self was drastically different from that of Moyes's childhood neighbors. Moyes's book is really a tribute to the ordinary people of faith who influenced his life—his dentist, the woman who helped him learn how to read, the local fruit grower—all of whom moved Moyes along in his faith journey, not through amazing ministries, out-of-this-world miracles, or radical acts, but by the way they went about their daily business with Christian integrity, humility, and dignity. They seemed to have a sense of self—a grasp of their true identities—that is missing today.

In many ways Moyes's book is sentimental, but it doesn't pass off a sanitized version of the past. Moyes tells of the trials of growing up with an alcoholic father and of the pain and struggle his father's addiction brought to his life. What struck me most, though, was the influence of Moyes's local family physician, a Dr. William Kemp, who had a profound impact not only on Moyes's life but on the entire local community. Dr. Kemp was a grocer until the age of thirty-eight, when he felt a call from God to become a medical doctor. For a man who had left school at the age of twelve, this was a difficult move. But Dr. Kemp persevered, and his studies took him to the United Kingdom to complete his medical training. He settled back in Australia in Box Hill and became a pillar of the community. Tragically, he became a widower when his young wife lost her life to an illness. He was heavily involved in his local church, ministering to young people and taking part in community groups. He eventually became the state president of his denomination. Dr. Kemp played a critical role in Moyes's life and conversion.

It was not unusual for Gordon Moyes's mother to ask him to go look for his alcoholic father, who would often be so drunk that he would collapse in the street and have to be carried home. One night in 1947, Gordon's mother asked him to help her look for his father, and they found him under a streetlight, lying prostrate in the gutter. Although this wasn't an unusual sight, this time his body was cold and stiff—he was dead. The family turned to the only person they could in this situation, Dr. Kemp. He came at once, comforted Mrs. Moyes, and fulfilled all of the necessary procedures for a deceased patient. He then took young Gordon Moyes outside to the washhouse to help him clean his shoes.

As Dr. Kemp scrubbed Gordon's shoes, he spoke of life and death, of the fact that young Gordon could not take over for his father but would now have new responsibilities for helping his mother and his family. He also spoke of eternity and heaven and of the need for Gordon to take responsibility for himself. This conversation became a turning point in Moyes's life. But this wasn't the only influence Dr. Kemp would have on the Moyes family. He also cared for Moyes's brother as he died of rheumatic fever. Later Dr. Kemp would lay hands on Moyes as he was ordained for ministry. Moyes wrote of Dr. Kemp's influence:

> Respect. That is what everyone gave to Dr Kemp. . . . In an era when youth were growing more cheeky towards their elders and less respectful towards authority, I cannot remember one young person ever having anything but respect for Dr Kemp. . . . Respect. He earned it. He received many honours from the community, from the churches, and from the Queen who presented him with an O.B.E. When he died at the age of eighty-nine, the church and the surrounding streets were packed with huge crowds of people . . . My mind boggled that such a man could have such an influence for so much good on the lives of so many people. He certainly took a special interest in me and in my latter life when I became a preacher, he was

very proud and often said to other people that I was the son he always wanted to have. He died childless but, in fact, hundreds of us looked upon him as a father figure.[4]

As I went about my business doing ministry in my area for the next few days, I could not stop thinking about the story of Dr. Kemp. I asked myself, *Where are such people today, people whose faith gives them such a grasp of who they are?* I remember walking from my office to the local coffee stand through the same streets in which Dr. Kemp had worked and ministered. So much had changed. As I sat drinking my coffee, I looked across the street at the tribe of goth and emo kids who always sit in the same place every day, their consciousness of people's reactions to their deliberately shocking fashion almost palpable. I glanced into a streetwear shop offering hundreds of "uniforms" of hip re-invention to anyone thirteen to forty-five years old. A group of high school girls sauntered by trying to grab the attention of a group of young men; the girls' outward display of confident, per-formative sexuality was so aggressive it almost could have been bottled. Across the street, a group of young men in their twen-ties emerged into the sun like modern-day vampires from one of those LAN computer game places filled with row after row of PCs, providing a contemporary Colosseum of computer gaming. The young men stood out front, smoking, displaying carefully con-structed attitudes intended to communicate their cynical disdain for the outside world.

The world of Gordon Moyes's book seemed a million miles away from the reality of my world and my context for ministry. The book took place in the same streets where I minister, but I might as well have been reading a fantasy novel about an alien civ-ilization. The example of Dr. Kemp's Christian character and his grasp of his God-given identity felt even further away. It seemed almost passé, like some outmoded technology that had been stored away in a museum of irrelevant and slightly weird machines. Yet in truth, such examples are needed now more than ever.

I had met people like Dr. Kemp when I was a boy growing up in church, but most of them were elderly and almost certainly have passed away by now. I realized that you just don't meet Christians like Dr. Kemp anymore. Sure, I know heaps of believers who do great things, who are kind or compassionate or committed, but very few seem to have the quiet assurance of faith, sense of self, and example shown by everyday saints like Dr. Kemp. Yet the grasp on Christian identity that people like Dr. Kemp displayed is desperately needed today. People yearn to have such an under-standing of their God-given identity. In twenty-first-century contemporary Christianity, we don't even have language to effec-tively describe the sense of self held by people like Dr. Kemp. The only word I could find to describe these people who have become almost extinct in the contemporary imagination of faith is *holy*.

HOLY

I have come to passionately believe that if we are to regain an understanding of who we are, if we are to find our real identi-ties, we must rediscover what it is to be holy. If we are to rescue ourselves and our culture from the crisis of self, we must re-image ourselves in the image of God. We must return to the source of our identities. For centuries, the path that has been trod by mil-lions of believers on their journey toward their true selves is the path of holiness. Holiness is the key to understanding our true selves.

Holiness is one of the most out-of-fashion Christian teachings in our day and age. I would say that it is so out of fashion that you rarely hear about it. It is enough to make most people run in the opposite direction. *Holy*. The word conjures up so many images—some positive, many negative. Holy people are like those soldiers who defuse land mines: we admire them, we are glad they are out there, but we sure as heck don't want to be one of them ourselves. Part of the reason for this is that the majority of Christian young adults I meet seem to be facing an identity crisis. Some are shy about publicly claiming their faith. I remember when a major newspaper wanted to do a story about innovative churches in our city, and I needed to grab a bunch of young-adult believers on short notice to appear in a photo shoot for the article. As I called friends, one told me that a lot of people probably wouldn't want to be in the photo because it would "out" them as believers to their non-Christian coworkers and friends. They feared their social currency would plummet and their hipness would erode.

NO ONE WANTS TO BE A CHRISTIAN DORK

I often meet believers who seem passionate and open about their faith but who also have a great deal of insecurity about their faith that makes them feel the need to communicate to the world that they are just as hip and cool as the rest of the culture. The cry of the day is "I just want the world to know that you can be a Christian and be cool too." Behind this inane statement is the mistaken belief that millions of non-Christians are waiting for Christianity to get hip enough, and then they will convert. I witness all kinds of lengths to which believers go to convince some unseen audience of nonbelievers that they are "just like everyone else." It is as if the secular public is so traumatized by past public impressions of Christians that many Christians have generated a deep insecurity about the link between their faith and their public selves. No one wants to be the term I hear so often when ministering with young adults—a Christian dork. We have come to believe that taking on a public self of holiness, becoming more like God, and taking seriously our God-given identity are all a kind of social suicide.

HOLINESS IS WHOLENESS

Ultimately holiness is about wholeness. It is the journey toward finding out who we really are, toward being at peace with ourselves, others, and the world around us. Our culture pushes us toward fragmentation, toward a false projection of self, which creates a split in us between the private and the public. Holiness brings us back together. Holiness points us toward who we are really meant to be. However, we fear holiness; we have discarded it, saying it's too hard. The problem is that we have a skewed view of holiness. We see it as all about keeping tabs on our bad behavior. *If holiness is moving toward perfection*, we ask ourselves, *how on earth can we make ourselves perfect in this lifetime?* We think of our own lives and all our imperfections; we think of our culture and the ways that it aids our slips into sin. We see others who seem much more spiritual or together than us fail in their attempts at holiness, and we resign ourselves to the fact that we will remain imperfect. To reengage authentically with the path of holiness, to find our true identities, we need to work through some of the stereotypes of holiness that have made it so un-hip.

FIGHTING FOR YOUR RIGHT TO PARTY

As I wait at a red light, I look at the car in front of me and notice that the driver looks like a college student. On her rear window is a large sticker reading "Bad Girl," with the *l* in *girl* written as a devil's tail. You don't have to look far to see such stickers on the cars of young women everywhere. Our culture associates being bad with fun: the term *naughty* is now associated with sexual pleasure; ice cream advertisements encourage us to give in to temptation; motorcycle ads encourage us to be "bad." Why should you try to be good in a world where being naughty is the way you have fun? In fact, having fun by being naughty is almost celebrated as a countercultural act of freedom fighting.

A common theme in American popular culture is the recurring battle between those who wish to have fun and those who wish to stop them. Movie after movie tells the story of people fighting against "the system," be it the college jocks who have to fight the dean in order to stage their frat party, the teenagers who wish to go on a drunken road trip but are stopped by their puritanical parents, or the punks who fight back against corporate suits to score points for individuality. Time and time again, popular culture pits the pleasure-seeking "good guys" against those killjoys who wish to stop the party people from having a good time (which is normally equated with getting high, losing your virginity, throwing a wild dance party, or all of the above). By the end of the movie, it almost always is revealed that the killjoys and the pleasure deniers really just want to stop the fun because they are repressed and secretly jealous of the naughty pleasure the party people are experiencing. Pop culture analysts Joseph Heath and Andrew Potter comment on the way cinema pits the pleasure seekers against the repressed:

> The mere thought that others might be enjoying themselves, experiencing pleasure, escaping from the dull, drab conformity, is intolerable. . . . Having fun is the ultimate subversive act. This is an incredibly consistent theme in the popular culture—from the final dance sequence in *Footloose* to the infamous rave scene in *The Matrix Reloaded*—and yet it is so obviously wishful thinking.[5]

Heath and Potter go on to note that the struggle to experience naughty pleasures is treated by popular culture as something akin to the civil rights movement, that the struggle to be "bad" in the face of a mythical enemy who wants you to conform is a political struggle. "This is an extremely attractive thought. After all, the traditional work of political organizing is extremely demanding and tedious.... Playing in a band . . . taking drugs and having lots of wild sex certainly beat union organization as a way to spend the weekend."[6] Heath and Potter make the point that this cultural myth actually means that our society changes little. The hard work that is required to change unjust laws and policies, or the long-term commitment to community development that is needed to help the poor, does not look very "sexy" when compared to the mythology of a "party on" revolution of being bad. Thus, social systems don't change, and the irony is that the faux freedom fight of pleasure only serves to keep unjust structures in place. Sadly, I have seen this dynamic develop in the minds of some Christians who, having bought the cultural myth of the pleasure seekers versus the killjoys, begin to overlay this myth upon their struggles with church tradition. Instead of engaging in mission, helping the poor, or challenging church structures, they attempt to revitalize faith by pushing the limits of traditionally acceptable Christian behavior, thus convincing themselves that they are modernizing the faith, when in fact they are changing little and simply serving their own self-interests.

It shouldn't be a shock to find that we have convinced ourselves that to become holy is to lose our cultural currency, to sacrifice our ability to "fit in." It's not cool to be set apart; it's not sexy to be holy. We believe that we must choose one or the other, that becoming holy means giving up on trying to relate to the wider culture—a frightening prospect for those raised with the mind-set of the horizontal self, in which a sense of self is supplied by peers and society. So we give up on trying to be holy, or we try to be holy and give up on trying to relate to our wider culture. We create alternatives to holiness, ones that are less risky to our public profile.

SECULAR HOLINESS

Interestingly, while Christian holiness is passé, our secular culture cannot avoid other forms of rigid "holinesses" that attempt to regulate our behavior. We may think we are hip, laid-back, twenty-first-century people, but we can get pretty puritanical about certain behaviors today. Just take a look at the green movement sweeping the globe.

We may buy organic foods for our health or take measures to reduce our carbon footprint or drink fair-trade coffee—all great things to do. However, we should realize that a multimillion-dollar industry has created a consumer culture for people who want to feel less guilty about their lives. It is a corporate attempt to keep us giving in to our temptations and buying our way into pleasure while keeping our consciences clear. As Jess Worth illustrates, "So much of the ethical consumption boom focuses on luxury goods. . . . Their main impact is to make the shopper feel good—'I'm doing something for the planet!'—without having to change their lifestyle one bit, while the companies laugh all the way to the bank."[7] Yet the problem is that sometimes these good activities act as offsets to placate our guilt about the rest of our behavior. Instead of giving us hope that we can grow spiritually, when exercised just in and of themselves, they keep us in the same patterns of spiritual stagnation.

BAR-CODE FAITH

Holiness is fostered by spiritual growth. Spiritual growth, therefore, like holiness, has slipped off the radar for many of the

Christian young adults I encounter. Sure, some people want to get rid of bad habits, others wish to move forward in life, and others wish to develop a different spirituality than the one they grew up with, one that fits more snugly with their lifestyle. However, I find very few people wanting to grow into perfection. I wonder if many of us are happy to rest in the knowledge that we have been saved, that we have a spirituality based on getting across the line of salvation. We have convinced ourselves that all that matters is whether we are going to live with Jesus when we die, that nothing about our souls really matters in *this* life. We have the Jesus Club membership card in our wallets to be pulled out in moments of danger or suffering, but the rest of the time we get on with having fun and running our own lives. Christian philosopher Dallas Willard has called such a view of discipleship "bar-code faith."

> Think of the bar codes now used on goods in most stores. The scanner responds only to the bar code. It makes no difference what is in the bottle or package that bears it, or whether the sticker is on the "right" one or not. The calculator responds through its electronic eye to the bar code and totally disregards everything else. If the ice cream sticker is on the dog food, the dog food is ice cream, so far as the scanner knows or cares.[8]

Now, on one level, the bar-code analogy is correct. Christianity is a religion of grace, that is, the scandalous belief that acceptance of Jesus as Lord gives individuals pardon from whatever sins or wrongdoing they have perpetrated. However, Willard makes the point that if that is our only view of faith, if the journey of discipleship begins and ends with that salvation moment, then our behavior and life on earth matter very little. Willard continues:

The real question, I think, is whether God would establish a bar code type of arrangement at all. It is we who are in danger: in danger of missing the fullness of life offered to us. Can we seriously believe that God would establish a plan for us that essentially bypasses the awesome needs of present human life and leaves human character untouched? Would he leave us even temporarily marooned with no help in our kind of world, with our kinds of problems: psychological, emotional, social and global? Can we believe that the essence of Christian faith and salvation covers nothing but death and after? Can we believe that being saved really has nothing whatever to do with the kinds of persons we are?[9]

When we have a bar-code faith, in which the only real spiritual transformation that occurs within us happens at the moment of salvation, a number of possible scenarios emerge regarding the shape our faith and lives will take, all of which do little to aid us in our journey toward finding our true selves.

STAGNATION

Eric became a Christian when he was seventeen. High school was a difficult time for him, as he found himself struggling with a real fear of death. He ended up giving his life to the Lord at a Christian youth camp after a friend invited him along. As he prayed for Jesus to come into his life, he felt the fear of death leave him and knew that he had the gift of eternal life. Eric is now twenty-four. He attends church irregularly, maybe once a month. He would like to go more often, but he has a busy social life and often has other social events planned at the same time. Eric cannot think of the last time he read the Bible. On New Year's Day, he made a resolution to read a Christian book his friend recommended, but he just hasn't gotten around to it. He prays occasionally when he is facing a difficult time, but he can go days without thinking about his faith, let alone God.

Eric's story is a classic example of how a bar-code faith can create stagnation in our spiritual lives. All that matters is the moment of salvation. With that issue resolved, there is nothing for Eric to do. Spiritual growth becomes a chore—much like cleaning the gutters—that keeps getting put off and put off. Eric remains a nice guy. He probably doesn't get involved in activities that will seriously damage his life, but slowly, inch by inch, spiritual stagnation begins to set in. It's like being slowly crushed by a glacier; it may take years, if not decades, but eventually a kind of spiritual death takes over. It's like the husband and wife who take their marriage for granted—one day they look at each other across the breakfast table and realize they feel nothing for each other. They can't think back to a fight, an affair, or an issue that has ruined their love, but they have slowly, breath by breath, strangled the life out of their relationship through neglect.

Literally millions of Christians are living like this. Sitting in churches around the world, they keep attending out of obligation or habit. Most are nice, pleasant people, but their faith neither excites them nor has any real impact on their lives. For many of these people, spiritual stagnation will lead to a kind of spiritual paralysis. They have no hope of moving toward their true selves in this life.

DETERIORATION

Ricardo has always been a Christian. He grew up in a large church, and his parents have always encouraged him to have Christian friends and to avoid what they call "sinful influences." Yet Ricardo has always had a heart to see his friends come to know the peace he feels from his relationship with Jesus. In senior high he asked four of his friends to an evangelistic service at his church. Three of them came, but as an evangelistic endeavor, it turned into a disaster. They giggled at the worship, the sermon was off topic, and the pastor kept referring to "we Christians." The whole experience seemed to turn off his friends from faith completely. This experience made Ricardo passionate about bridging the gap between church and the culture in which his friends lived.

Ricardo began to immerse himself in his friends' culture in order to relate more effectively to them. He began listening to their music and hanging out with them at parties. He realizes his friends have no real interest in church or spiritual matters, even though he now goes to a more laid-back church that meets in a café. One of his friends came once and didn't mind it, but he hasn't come back. Ricardo is determined not to be a Ned Flanders type of Christian, like many of the people he grew up with. He has started questioning various Christian teachings and has noticed that his behavior is changing. He tries to avoid giving people the clichéd Christian answer, but this just means that sometimes he says nothing. As Ricardo looks at his life, he realizes that he set out to influence his friends, but they have ended up influencing him more. His friends see no difference between his life and theirs. Increasingly Ricardo doesn't know what he believes.

Possessing a bar-code faith can result in another scenario: deterioration. With salvation a given, and no spiritual growth to guide life, often faith doesn't just stagnate but deteriorates. Bar-code faith tells us that our earthly behavior is ultimately of no consequence. When we believe that because we are saved, nothing we do matters, inevitably our behavior suffers. I've observed this train of thought as I've worked in young-adult ministry. I believe it is one of the key reasons so many young adults abandon the faith. If you live in a culture that celebrates hedonism, and if you are taught a bar-code faith, is it any wonder that the lives of so many young adults look no different from those of their non-Christian friends?

As in the story of Ricardo, I have often seen faith deteriorate among those who attempt to evangelize their friends by bridging the cultural divide between their non-Christian friends and Christian culture. With no framework of Christian growth aside from bar-code faith and with no theology of holiness to transform their lives, they find themselves being transformed by secular culture. Instead of discovering their true identities, they find themselves being rebranded by the culture.

SEPARATION

Simon would be described by some of his coworkers as holy. The problem is that they don't mean it as a compliment. Simon spends most of his lunch breaks with the two other Christians from his workplace. He finds the attitudes of many of his nonbelieving coworkers to be a negative influence, so he chooses to be apart from them. Simon spends most of his time outside of work at church activities. He is an avid fan of Christian music and prefers to watch Christian cable rather than regular television. Simon plays basketball for his church team, which is part of a Christian league. He also works out at a Christian gym. He recently bought his car from a Christian dealer, which he found in a Christian business directory. He is part of a Christian group concerned about what he calls "the increasing secularization of culture." The group plans to get more Christian candidates elected to governmental offices. He cannot name one non-Christian friend whom he would invite over for dinner.

Sometimes those with a bar-code faith seem to want to leave earth and enter a kind of proxy heaven before they die. They attempt to flee any kind of temptation by avoiding the world. Christians living within the framework of separation see life on earth as simply too depraved and beyond repair, and thus they are encouraged to pursue a spirituality in which they hide from any negative influences. While such a framework may in some ways keep people from trouble, this positive effect comes at a cost. Any chance of transforming the world is negated. The good news is hidden away from those who need it. Separation also means that the faith we develop is nurtured in a vacuum; it has no chance to develop spiritual "antibodies." As soon as it comes into contact with a virus, a full-blown infection can develop. Instead of moving toward their true selves, those who take on a spirituality of separation become images of what they think a Christian should be. Sadly, this image often reeks of the religiosity that Jesus condemned in the religious gatekeepers of his day.

SACRED BUBBLES

The problem is that so much of the teaching and instruction we receive about holiness happens in places that are almost like spiritual vacuums. They are like the operating theaters in hospitals, where everything is disinfected and people wear masks and gowns to protect them from the infections of real life. Changing your life seems easy during the altar call, when everyone is down front crying and hugging. Moving toward perfection seems possible at the convention, seminary, camp, or festival. Most of the information we receive is in Sunday morning church services. This information, if not forgotten by lunchtime, usually stays simply that—information. It is rarely applied and thus becomes a powerful force in making us feel guilty and ineffective.

If we look through church history, we see people who were labeled holy, yet their holiness seems to have an otherworldly quality about it that we could never achieve. Take, for example, the early church saint Simeon the Stylite. Simeon lived from AD 390 to 459 and was renowned for his self-denying (some would say masochistic) spirituality. Simeon would fast for incredible lengths. He also would wear a girdle under his clothes that would inflict tremendous pain to the point that the girdle would mesh with his wounds. He would even stand for days at a time in order to "deny his flesh." But Simeon would be remembered most by history for his attempts to free himself from the distractions and temptations of the world by living his life on a small platform at the top of a pole. Some will argue that this was a prophetic action against the increasing spiritual corruption of his culture, but nevertheless his brand of spirituality betrays a dangerous thread of thought concerning separation and holiness within Christianity, one that has warped our view of spiritual growth. But Simeon is not alone. Julian of Norwich lived in a small, sealed-off room; St. Francis of Assisi pushed a worm into a bodily wound to eat at his flesh.

Many past saints were influenced by a worldview that saw the material world as evil and as something to retreat from. That's why so many of them fled to the desert or the wilderness or to monasteries. While some of these saints became literal martyrs, others saw their separation from the world for the sake of holiness as a kind of martyrdom. Thus, it is little wonder that many young adults look at holiness as a form of social death.

While many of us today would not wish to flee to the desert, we still carry the same view of the world inside us. We create a modern version of their deserts—a place where we try to live out our faith in isolation from the world. It could be that we end up living in a kind of Christian social ghetto, in which we listen only to Christian music, watch only Christian cable, read only Christian books, and spend most of our free time only with Christians. But the track record shows us that living in such a ghetto doesn't at all protect us from our more dangerous and destructive habits. Such a practice is based around the idea that it is the world and nonbelievers who are sinful and potentially destructive, and if we can just separate ourselves from "them," we will be okay. The Bible, however, teaches a different truth: we all have the potential to commit evil and to be controlled by sin.

Sadly, Christians have proven that sin can and does happen in the Christian ghetto; it just usually happens behind closed doors. Such dualistic views of holiness seem millions of miles away from the reality of our lives and our spiritual capabilities. These views are based on a worldview of escape and detachment. Biblical faith, in contrast, gives us a spirituality based on struggle and engagement. Therefore, we need a more robust approach to holiness, one that takes seriously the temptations that we face daily, one that recognizes that we are capable of acting in destructive ways, one that doesn't require us to flee the mission field to which Jesus sent us, and one that doesn't require us to abandon our ordinary lives to achieve spiritual growth.

A philosophy of holiness that is based in a framework of separation simply ends up glorifying spiritual heavyweights who never seem to struggle with genuine temptation. This is no good for us either. To walk the path of holiness and to find our true selves, we need to rediscover a biblical holiness grounded in the value of creation.

CHAPTER 10

Meeting Your Future Self

As Christians, we need to practice a holiness rooted in the biblical notions of creation and re-creation. For too long, Christian holiness has been defined by its dualism, the tendency to divide the world into good and bad, spirit and matter, saint and sinner. We need to embrace the original biblical idea of holiness that emerges from the story of Creation. To understand a holiness of re-creation, and to discover a true sense of self, we must return to the scene of the first creation in Genesis 1. We find in Genesis an insight into the intentions of God:

> God saw all that he had made, and it was very good. (v. 31)

Though it might seem obvious at first, this statement is actually quite radical. By claiming that creation is good, the Bible places itself in contrast to a number of other religions and philosophies that hold that this earth upon which we live is, at best, irrelevant or, at worst, evil. However, biblical faith declares that the world God has made is good. Creation is very good; it is not evil. It is the environment in which God created us to prosper and thrive. Sadly, many of the marks of a separationist holiness are a result of forgetting that God created his world good. As Christianity moved away from its Jewish roots, its followers abandoned key elements of its spiritual heritage and instead looked to Greek philosophy, which saw matter and creation as fundamentally flawed. But Genesis 1 tells us that creation was intended to be good, and so were we. God never intended to create a world of matter and then destroy it so that we could "graduate" to some superior spiritual plane. Rather, this world is the home that God created for us to live in with him and the whole of creation.

YOU ARE A WORK OF ART

When God created you, you were an integral part of his panoramic plan to create a home for him. This home is the greatest work of art ever created (or even imagined). As God dreamed of what the cosmos and the creation would be like, as he sketched out distant planets, the human smile, complex jungle ecosystems, the humpback whale, and the bird-of-paradise, you were part of his creation. He imagined you as you should be. You and your development are just as key to his plan as the Andes Mountains and the platypus are. You are a vital and irreplaceable element of God's good creation. That's why he is so passionately committed to seeing you become the person you were meant to be. Your movement toward your true self, toward the whole person God wants you to be, is part of his plan to remake creation according to his original design. That's why he calls you forward toward him to find your true name written on the white stone he holds in his hand.

CREATED IN GOD'S IMAGE

In the midst of his creation, which was very good, God placed creatures that were very different from all the other creatures he had made. These creatures were created in his image. Theologian Richard Middleton, in his book *The Liberating Image*,[1] notes that the term "image of God" was an incredibly radical way of describing humanity. Israel spent much of its early history living on the edge of more powerful cultures, such as the Sumerians and the Babylonians. These cultures saw humans as slaves whose only role was to ensure that the gods' needs were met. They saw the universe as a kind of concentration camp in which humans worked to satisfy the needs and desires of capricious gods. The Israelites, in contrast, dared to believe that God created humans to partner with him in cultivating and blessing creation. Holiness was not mindless devotion through repetitive rituals designed to placate angry gods. Rather, it was cooperating with God in the endeavor of improving creation. And so we begin to detect part of our original identity. We don't need to find ourselves; rather, we need to rediscover our original purpose by imitating God's creative endeavors in making the world a better place.

It is also vital to note that Genesis, contrary to popular belief, does not say creation was made perfect. It says that it was "very good." One of the great mysteries of faith is that God chooses us to partner with him in making creation, which is very good, perfect.

I remember as a boy helping my father paint our house. I'm sure he could have accomplished the task by himself, but he chose to teach me how to paint. By involving me in the process (leaving sections of the house for me to complete), he honored me as someone who was able to contribute. This is what God does with us. He invites us to join him in making creation whole. The essence of holiness, after all, is wholeness. However, there is a problem.

MAKING THINGS BETTER VERSUS
MAKING THINGS WORSE

Now, the Bible makes clear that the story doesn't end here. Creation doesn't just happen and then everyone lives happily ever after. No, humans are both blessed and cursed with the gift of free will. We choose not to embrace our God-given identity; instead, we pursue our own agendas separate from God. We possess tremendous power; we can improve the world and our lives through cooperation with God, or we can bring injustice, destruction, and death into the world through our insistence on relying not on God but on our own abilities and power.

How often do we see this reality in our own lives? Often we do good; we improve life on earth (even in the smallest ways). Yet other times we only bring division, anger, and violence into this world. This is one of the classic human dilemmas: God's image-bearers, commissioned with the task of making all things better, are making things worse. But God has a solution. God intends to re-create the world.

THE MESSIAH COMES

God came into the world in the form of a carpenter. His mission was to illustrate to us how we are to live as image-bearers of God. He lived a life of holiness, a life that improved the world, that brought a world struggling under the burden of sin, corruption, and death back to its original purpose to give glory to God. Through his life, death, and resurrection, Jesus showed us the way to be truly human, to be truly "the image of God."

Genesis tells us that Adam was created from the dust of the earth. The Gospels show us how Jesus became the new Adam. He was placed in the dirt of the grave, yet through the miracle of resurrection, a new kind of life was breathed into him, a new kind of human was born, one who will lead us in God's task of remaking creation whole. The amazing thing is that God intends to make *us* whole and perfect as well. The crux of this remaking of ourselves happens as we come into relationship with Christ.

It is interesting to note that when some people in the Bible encountered Jesus, they were given a new name, like the name we will be given on the white stone mentioned in Revelation 2:17. Simon became Peter, and Saul became Paul. Paul says in his letter to the Colossians, "Once you were alienated from God and were enemies in your minds because of your evil behavior. But now he has reconciled you by Christ's physical body through death to present you holy in his sight, without blemish and free from accusation" (1:21–22). This reconciliation with Christ is key. Paul is stating unequivocally that the source of life for the whole of creation is Christ. Christ is life. Therefore, if we are to rediscover who we really are, we must find the blueprint of who we are meant to be in the person of Christ. He is the new Adam, the first human. He is the image in which humanity is made. To become ourselves, we first must become more like Christ.

> The Son is the image of the invisible God, the firstborn over all creation. For in him all things were created: things in heaven and on earth, visible and invisible, whether thrones or powers or rulers or authorities; all things have been created through him and for him. He is before all things, and in him all things hold together. (Col. 1:15–17)

Think about this: our identities have been replaced with images. Our culture cannot tell us who we really are; instead, we are given the disposable images of the media landscape. We desperately search for a sense of self, but our culture leads us into a hall of mirrors. Yet Paul is introducing us to a different kind of image: the image of Christ, the first image, the only true image, the image that trumps all of the false images of our culture, the image that forms the spiritual DNA of the whole of creation. The image of Christ is kind of like the picture on a jigsaw puzzle box. Our culture offers us no finished picture to help us complete the puzzle of our identity; instead, it merely offers us a jumbled mess of puzzle pieces, which we constantly configure, reconfigure, and then deconstruct. But the image of Christ offers us the ultimate image of wholeness, pointing us toward our true self-image.

ENEMIES OF THE IMAGE OF CHRIST

We have two choices before us. We can attempt to find a sense of self in the patterns of this world, or we can put our trust in the source of our true identity. Just as in Paul's day, our culture today offers competing visions of self. The "powers and principalities" exist in our time just as they did when Paul was writing.

Basing your identity on the image of Christ was and is a radical act. Theologians Brian Walsh and Sylvia Keesmaat[2] note that heeding Paul's call to take on the image of Christ was an extremely countercultural and potentially dangerous thing for believers living in the Roman Empire to do. Everywhere in the public and private spaces of the Roman world, imperial imagery was communicated. This imagery was the empire's reminder that Rome and Caesar were the source of the people's well-being. To root your identity in the image of Christ was to say that you put your faith in Christ, not Caesar, for provision and meaning. Such a statement would have been deeply subversive. The Roman Empire promoted an alternative vision of self, just as the multiheaded media empire of our day offers us ways of being that are opposed to the image of Christ. Therefore, Paul's warning to the believers in Colossae also rings true for us:

> See to it that no one takes you captive through hollow and deceptive philosophy, which depends on human tradition and the elemental spiritual forces of this world rather than on Christ.
>
> For in Christ all the fullness of the Deity lives in bodily form, and in Christ you have been brought to fullness. . . . God made you alive with Christ. (Col. 2:8–10, 13)

DAILY ASSAULTS ON YOUR GOD-GIVEN IDENTITY

My office is next to a mall, and each day as I was writing this book, I would walk to the mall to get a sandwich for lunch. On the way, I would notice challenge after challenge of who I am meant to be: billboards, the public acts of others, the images on television screens, "lifestyle" and "personality" products for sale—all offered me an alternative vision of myself. As soon as you put down this book, unless you are reading it in the middle of a desert, you will most likely find your God-given identity being challenged in some way. Therefore, we have to ask ourselves how much we want to claim our God-given identity in this life. Remember, I'm not talking about works or salvation; I'm talking about how much we want to become our true selves in this life.

THREE CHOICES

We have three choices. We can move toward becoming the true version of ourselves, we can stay where we are, or we can go backward. If we take seriously Jesus' claim in Luke 4:19 that the year of the Lord's favor is here and that God's kingdom is breaking out in the world, it makes sense that Jesus' teachings about how to live have a point. His instructions for living were not just spiritual fairy floss that he spouted before he got down to the real deal of dying on the cross and coming back to life. If Jesus' way is *the* way, and if that way is breaking out in our time, and if that way is going to be the only way in the future, it makes sense that we must begin to change ourselves now in preparation for the future. In fact, the more we become the people God created us to be in perfection, the more we will find our lives filled with meaning.

Holiness is not about pointless and impossible perfectionism. It is about becoming the people we are meant to be. It is the ultimate discovery of our true selves. Each step toward holiness brings us closer to becoming who we really are. Each step away from holiness causes us to lose more of our sense of self. As the great Christian thinker C. S. Lewis wrote, "The goal towards which He is beginning to guide you is absolute perfection; and no power in the whole universe, except you yourself can prevent Him from taking you to that goal."[3] This is not just talk; this is about your life.

IT'S YOUR LIFE, STUPID!

When Bill Clinton ran for president of the United States against George Bush in 1992, one of his campaign slogans was "It's the economy, stupid." Clinton used the statement to highlight the importance of the economy in the election.

The same point needs to be made in regard to holiness: it's your life, stupid! Not just your eternal lives, but your everyday lives also. When it comes to holiness, we must make the point that it is not just an abstract theological concept. The pursuit of holiness is about the quality of our lives. Believers often miss this fact. We understand the effect that sin has on our relationship with God, but too often we fail to understand the polluting effect that sin has on our happiness and quality of life. Thus, Christian tradition has distinguished between justification and sanctification. As theologian Anthony A. Hoekema explains: "In justification . . . the guilt of our sin is removed on the basis of the atoning work of Christ. By pollution, however, we mean the corruption of our nature. . . . In sanctification the pollution of sin is in the process of being removed (though it will not be totally removed until the life to come)."[4] Those who call on the name of Christ are saved from the eternal consequences of sin. However, by becoming followers of Christ, we don't automatically find the caustic effects of sin removed from our lives.

EXPLODING POTTED PLANTS

When my wife and I moved into our house, we discovered that the previous occupants (who were lovely people) left a potted kumquat tree for us on the back deck. The plant was a beautiful feature as we looked out into our backyard, and it also provided constant fruit. Because it was something we valued, I made sure I watered and fed the plant regularly.

One morning I was standing out on the back deck with a cup of coffee, deep in thought. I happened to look over at the potted plant, and, to my disbelief, the pot containing the plant exploded. Within a millisecond it disintegrated. Dirt went everywhere, all over our deck. The tree was ruined.

Unbeknownst to me, over a period of several years, the wooden pot had been rotting. Slowly but surely it had been losing structural integrity. The destruction was incremental until the morning the pot simply fell apart. This is how sin works: it causes a slow death. Holiness is the task of working against this gradual degradation of life.

It is totally possible for us to be in a saving relationship with Christ but to see our quality of life dulled, degraded, or even destroyed by the effects of sin. However, many of us don't see this. We think only of the eternal ramifications of our sin. We are unaware of sin's corrosive influence on our sense of identity and on our ability to live the sort of lives we want to live. The more we allow sin to infiltrate our lives, the more we move away from our true selves. Thus, by choosing the path of holiness, by moving toward our true selves, we are simply deciding to live a life that is both functional and fulfilling. As Christian writer Richard Foster notes, "A holy life is a life that works."[5]

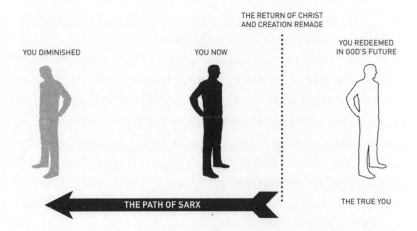

WHEN LIFE SARX

The fourteenth-century English mystic Walter Hilton wrote clearly of the choice between accepting our true selves, which he described as being branded in the image of the Trinity of God, and accepting our unredeemed selves, or being branded in the image of "the wretched trinity." Hilton explained this "wretched trinity" in a letter he wrote to a young woman to help her along her faith journey. In the letter, he compared our choice to accept or reject God's original purpose with Adam's choice in the garden.

This was the original nature of the human soul, this the dignity, status and honour which God intended for it. This was the status you had in Adam, before man committed his first sin. But when Adam sinned, choosing to love and take pleasure in himself, he lost this honour and dignity in its entirety, as you did in him, and he fell from the holy trinity in to a foul, disgusting wretched trinity—a state of forgetfulness of God, ignorance of him and an animal lust for himself.[6]

The same choice confronts us today, and the ramifications of the choice we make can be just as serious. Hilton points out that when we embrace the false self as Adam did, we lose our honor and dignity. We bring upon ourselves a kind of self-judgment in which we fall into a forgetfulness of God, an ignorance of the fact that God is the source of all life. Cut off from this source, we find our behavior becoming less human and more animalistic. This is what happens when we give ourselves over to what Paul describes often as "the flesh." But for centuries we have misinterpreted "the flesh" as our actual bodies and our bodily needs, desires, and functions. This kind of anti-body holiness, which is rooted in a separationist worldview, has led many of our great saints and heroes of the faith to declare war on their bodies.

When Paul, writing in Greek, penned the word we translate as "flesh," he used the Greek word *sarx*. To describe our physical bodies, he used the word *soma*, which is most often translated as "body." But instead of indicating just the physical body, *sarx* refers to material things that are corruptible and temporary. New Testament theologian N. T. Wright illuminates for us Paul's use of the term *flesh* or *sarx*: "For him, the word 'flesh' is a way of denoting material within the corruptible world and drawing attention to the fact that it is precisely corruptible, that it will decay and die."[7]

Thus, the path of holiness is about ridding ourselves of *sarx*, that is, anything in life—attitudes, relationships, actions, desires, or worldviews—that carries with it the spirit of death and corruption, that moves against God's intention for the world. Imagine Paul's plea to rid ourselves of our flesh as a plea to rid ourselves of that which is not our true self. For example, casual sex carries with it the spirit of *sarx*. By sleeping with people with whom we have no binding, covenantal relationship, we end up using them as commodities through which to satiate ourselves. This outcome may not be immediately apparent; in fact, a casual sexual encounter may initially seem thrilling and satisfying. But that misses the point. The spirit of *sarx* is corrosive; that is, its effects wear at us over a long time. Treat others as commodities rather than humanizing them, and ultimately you find yourself becoming dehumanized by others or by yourself.

We understand this concept when it comes to fast food. You may love that quarter pounder, but you know that eating one for lunch and dinner every day will have a corrosive effect on your health. If you continue such a diet, the effects on your life and health will intensify. Likewise, the spirit of *sarx* can impact many areas of our lives. When our lives are filled with anger and judgment, our health suffers. Studies show that people who are stressed and angry are far more susceptible to diseases such as heart disease and cancer. In my book *The Trouble with Paris*, I examine the ways in which our hyper-consumerist lifestyle can bring the spirit of *sarx* upon both our spirituality and our general well-being. When we choose to ignore the biblical mandate of caring for the poor and the marginalized, we bring the spirit of *sarx* upon ourselves and even the larger culture. This theme recurs throughout the Old Testament.

An understanding of the biblical concept of *sarx* changes how we view both judgment and holiness. When we choose not to embrace our true images, our redeemed selves, and look for our identity in other places, we bring the spirit of *sarx* upon ourselves. N. T. Wright explains:

> The failure of human beings to be the truly image-bearing creatures God intended results, therefore, in corruption and death. . . . We can see clearly that the frequently repeated warnings about sin and death . . . are not arbitrary as though God was simply a tyrant inventing odd laws and losing his temper with those who flouted them, but structural.[8]

This understanding is essential. Too many of us think of God as an angry tyrant; in truth, God is a loving guide instructing us in the way that life works.

If I were to go to the snake habitat at the zoo, ignore the warning signs, and place my arm into the poisonous snakes' cage, I would most likely be bitten. But I would be foolish to accuse the zookeeper of training the snakes to bite me. We know that if you place your arm into the cage of a deadly snake, it will almost certainly bite you. That is how the system works. It is, as N. T. Wright says, structural. The zookeeper has two options: either he can close down the zoo and thus deprive us of the joy of seeing the animals, or he can allow us to come to the zoo but post warning signs informing us how we can best enjoy the animals in a safe manner.

This is how holiness works. When Paul speaks of *sarx* and urges us to take on the image of Christ, he is simply erecting a warning sign that tells us to follow the path marked by life and creation rather than one filled with the spirit of death and destruction. So when we worship God, when we base the whole of our lives around the image of Christ, we find life. When we look elsewhere for our identity, we enter into a worship of things apart from God—we become idolaters and thus fill our lives with a spirit of death.

Wright continues, "Humans were made to function in particular ways, with worship of the creator as the central feature, and those who turn away from that worship . . . are thereby opting to seek life where it is not to be found, which is another way of saying that they are courting their own decay and death."[9] When we take on the false self, when we create a self based solely on surface image and publicity, we bring the spirit of *sarx* upon our lives. We choose to walk away from our true selves and head in the opposite direction. We turn our backs on the potential of finding happiness and meaning.

A CULTURE OF GOLLUMS

Part of the structure of the way life works is that we become what we love. If we love that which is "of the flesh"—that which is corrupt, passing, and diminished—we ourselves become those things. We become something like Gollum, the character in the Lord of the Rings trilogy. He is no longer himself. He is torn between two personalities; his lower self has almost completely taken over his higher self. He is a shattered, mutated version of what he used to be, living in the shadows of the world. He has become his own lust for his "precious," the ring that symbolizes his desire for power.

I was interested to discover that some have speculated that the inspiration for the character Gollum comes from a Jewish cautionary folktale of the Golem. In the tale a rabbi attempts to create a human the way God created Adam, by breathing life into clay in order to protect his community from anti-Semitic attacks. He manages to create a form of life; however, as the rabbi is not God, his creation does not bear the image of God. His creation is alive—it is clay come to life—yet it is a monster named Golem.

The author Mary Shelley modernized the Golem myth when she wrote her classic tale, *Frankenstein*. Frankenstein attempts to create a human using, not his spiritual powers, but science. Like the rabbi, he creates a monster rather than a human.

The message of these three stories is clear: the further we move away from our divinely given image, the less human we become. Worship God and become like him; worship other things and become them. When we take on a false self or a media mask, we initially try to use it to our advantage. But the more we come to rely on it, the more it controls us. We become it. We may still appear to be ourselves, but we have become parodies of ourselves. We are the same people, but through our obsession with our false selves, we have turned into poor imitations of who we were meant to be.

I remember walking down Rodeo Drive in Los Angeles past some women who'd undergone way too much plastic surgery. They were probably attractive women in their youth, but their faces now were a parody of beauty, an exaggerated, ridiculous version of their former selves. Their obsession with their public image of beauty had become their Gollum.

By looking to Christ as our primary image-giver, we find our true selves. As with anything of worth, the journey toward our true selves is not easy. Yet there is no other real option for people who wish to live lives of meaning, fulfillment, joy, and worth. We don't find our true selves overnight. Holiness is a process, a goal toward which to strive.

A NATION CALLED TO FIND THEIR TRUE SELVES

We see this process of holiness in the story of Israel. God called his people for a special purpose. Israel was to be a holy people whose embodiment of God's values would speak to the nations of the world. He called Israel to be a living example of the way he wanted the world to be. They were the foretaste of his coming reign. However, if you look at the history of Israel, again and again they fail to live up to their calling. The prophets remind them of who they are meant to be. The prophets' words are a reminder of God's purpose and how the people are meant to act—they are words of rebuke, a challenge to move toward God's design for them. The amazing thing is that God allows Israel to struggle. Although there are moments of spectacular divine intervention, the main way God moves his people toward holiness is through everyday, sweat-and-blood struggle.

Israel is called to become holy by following the Torah. *Torah* means "instructions." Often people who read the Torah for the first time are shocked. They may start out expecting heavenly panoramas and celestial mysteries, but instead they are presented with practical instructions for living, which even touch on such topics as farming accidents, menstruation, and mildew. This emphasis on real life shows us that revolution happens through a million miniscule decisions. Humans tussle with the earthly temptations of sex, jealousy, anger, envy, and greed. That's why Paul wrote:

> Put to death, therefore, whatever belongs to your earthly nature: sexual immorality, impurity, lust, evil desires and greed, which is idolatry. Because of these, the wrath of God is coming. You used to walk in these ways, in the life you once lived. But now you must also rid yourselves of all such things as these: anger, rage, malice, slander, and filthy language from your lips. Do not lie to each other, since you have taken off your old self with its practices and have put on the new self, which is being renewed in knowledge in the image of its Creator. (Col. 3:5–10)

These instructions for behavior are not there because God is a prude or a killjoy. They are there because God understands that the transformation of the world begins with the day-to-day choices of his people. At first, this suggestion seems almost ludicrous, but you just have to spend half an hour reading through the book of Leviticus to see how seriously God takes his approach. God knows the world can't change unless we change. We can donate all the money in the world to the poor, but until corruption is wiped out, little will change. We can hold as many peace summits as we want, but without a spirit of forgiveness, the circle of violence only continues. Yet miraculously God chooses for us to aid him in his mission to transform creation, and the starting point for that transformation begins with the human will, with the harnessing of our desires. Does it sound strange that the Creator of the universe is interested in our human wants and desires? Don't be fooled: God is happy to get his hands dirty in the quest to help us put on the new self.

DIRTY HOLINESS

The earthiness of holiness in the Bible is quite astounding, especially when compared to other religions. We find refreshingly ordinary people struggling with all-too-familiar temptations and situations. Compared to Hollywood's storytelling, the reportage of the Bible is brutally realistic and stunningly honest. Just think of David, Israel's most beloved king, the branch from which Christ the Messiah would come. We encounter David not as a cardboard figure who easily fits into the category of good or bad, but as a man who is frighteningly like us. He is a man who is capable of deep holiness—the writer of Psalms, the defeater of Goliath—but he is also the peeping Tom who stares at Bathsheba from his rooftop and then conspires to have her husband killed in battle so that he can bed her freely.

Also in the Bible we find Peter, that fantastically bullheaded character, the person upon whom God in human form declares that he will build his people. We find this pillar of the church brandishing weapons, chopping off ears, and constantly getting it wrong. He is even called "Satan" by Jesus himself.

These are not people we would call "Christian Dorks"; these are complex, flawed characters just like us. Often their potential for wrongdoing seems equal to their propensity for good. We see that their very human desires and impulses lead them away from God's designs for their lives.

This is true of so many of the people to whom I minister. It is true of myself. We all desperately want to move toward our true selves, but our desires, egos, and impulses derail our attempts. Our culture doesn't have answers for the conflicts that we feel over our desires. God, however, views our desires as his workshop. He doesn't remove them; instead, he encourages us to redeem them, to use them as fuel to move toward our true self.

MASTERING YOUR DESIRES

Many of us struggle to understand how to control the powerful forces within us that we call *desires*. Sure, we want to move toward becoming the perfect, redeemed people God wants us to be, but we also realize that we are filled with desires and impulses that seem to take us away from our true selves. Part of the problem lies in the way we, as Christians, have dealt with our desires: we have been encouraged to either ignore them or completely repress them. Yet when we repress something, we know it usually returns with more force or pops up in another place or in another form. And so we end up more confused. We are also confused because our culture gives us mixed messages about how to deal with our deepest wants and impulses.

DOING WHAT YOU WANT

We like to think we live in a civilized culture. We have roads, health care, and jobs that pay. However, these things come at a cost. In order to have them, we must go to work, pay taxes, be responsible, be good. When the alarm clock goes off in the morning to wake you in time to get to work, you can hit the snooze button and stay in bed, but you will face the consequences. You won't get paid that day; you might even lose your job.

In one episode of *The Simpsons*, a popular TV psychologist comes to Springfield. Homer and Marge, who are concerned about their son Bart's bad behavior, attend the taping of the psychologist's show to get some parenting advice. But to their surprise, Brad Goodman, the psychologist, encourages the citizens to embrace their "inner child" and follow Bart's example of doing what they feel like. At first, this advice turns out to be great fun for the citizens of Springfield. However, things go wrong when a local government worker decides not to adequately assemble a stand of bleachers; when the bleachers fill up with a crowd, several people are injured. When questioned, the worker explains that he has been caught up in the current mood and chose not to assemble the bleachers properly because he didn't feel like it. The episode is a clever illustration of the tensions we feel when it comes to our desires.[10]

On one hand, we realize that we must follow the rules to have a peaceful and well-run society; on the other hand, all of us struggle with the desire to do what we want. The rules of society are based on being civil and tolerant toward others, showing community spirit, and acting responsibly, yet we often have contrasting feelings. Sometimes we feel powerful urges to yell at people, to have sex with people we are not married to, or to eat large amounts of junk food that we know isn't good for our bodies. Sometimes we don't want to follow society's rules: we don't want to be civil to others; we don't want to be responsible. Sometimes, in order to feel better, we manipulate or lie to or use others. Thus, we find within ourselves a battle. We know to fit into society we must follow the rules, yet many of the desires welling up in us contradict the rules.

FOLLOWING YOUR DESIRES VERSUS FOLLOWING THE RULES

Ian is in his late twenties. He works hard and has a young family and a wife he loves. One night, as he makes the long commute home in his car, he listens to his favorite talk-radio station. The commentator makes a lot of sense to Ian. He speaks of the need to return to a past when people cared for each other, when neighbors said hello and knew each other by name. The commentator blames the current isolation in society on the breakdown of the family and the general lack of values in our culture, including the spread of pornography. Ian finds himself nodding in agreement. The commentator also gives good investment advice and parenting tips, all of which Ian takes note of and puts into practice.

Later that night, after his wife and children go to bed, Ian unwinds by channel surfing. For a few minutes he watches a music video he liked when he was in college. In the video the singer stands atop a smashed police car with a baseball bat in hand. Ian's mind goes back to the freedom he felt at that time. For a second he feels a sense of nostalgia for his wild college days, and he also guiltily begins to feel trapped in his role as father. The music video ends, and a late-night advertisement for a sex line comes on. Ian finds himself watching the young woman in the ad as he makes a mental note of the number. Looking across the room at the telephone, Ian considers for a second whether he should call. He jumps up and heads to bed, feeling very frustrated and guilty and wondering if his life is heading in the wrong direction.

It's easy to feel some sympathy for Ian. He is a man who, like many of us, is caught between his rational beliefs about what it means to be a good father, husband, and citizen, and his desire to call the sex chat line. He finds himself frustrated by his family responsibilities. Many of us feel this way. Ian's story shows us how we receive differing messages from the media. We hear messages encouraging us to work hard, to get a good education, to exercise, to eat healthily, and to think of others and the environment. Yet we hear other messages encouraging us to buy pornography, to gamble, and to drink the weekend away. Thus, we find ourselves in a tug-of-war between these competing messages.

We also feel this tension as we receive contradictory messages from our culture. On one hand, we are told, "Obey the rules and you will find success, achievement, and meaning." On the other hand, we are told, "Obey your desires and you will find pleasure, happiness, and meaning." These two conflicting pieces of advice form the basis of countless myths and stories told to us by popular culture. You've probably never really thought about them, but we are exposed to them all the time. To illustrate, I've concocted two movie story lines that I'm sure will sound quite familiar; no doubt you've heard these stories thousands of times.

FOLLOW THE RULES: TYPICAL MOVIE SCRIPT

Johnny is from the wrong side of the tracks. All around him people are making the wrong choices. But Johnny is a great football player despite being short. He works hard and resists the temptation to go partying with his neighborhood buddies. Against the odds, Johnny becomes the first player from his neighborhood to win a scholarship to a top football college. At first Johnny struggles: he struggles with his grades and with the other players, who don't accept him because of his background. But because of his hard work, determination, and grit, Johnny becomes a star player on the team.

With his new status, he is presented with some temptations to follow his desires and throw away the rules. First, he is tempted to leave his "girl next door" girlfriend, who loved him before his success, for a "sexy" seductress type who is only interested in his fame. Then he is tempted to enjoy some of the seedier trappings that come with success, including doing drugs and partying. He is even tempted to throw it all away by taking a bribe to throw a game. Johnny, although initially tempted, resists each of these temptations. Finally, he learns the lesson of teamwork and selflessly lets another teammate make the winning play, thus earning the respect of both his old neighborhood and his new teammates.

The message behind the movie is clear: resist your desires, work hard, be selfless, and you will win the respect of those around you and find success. Those are the rules.

FOLLOW YOUR DESIRES: TYPICAL MOVIE SCRIPT

Jenny is a girl from a small, tree-lined town. She is gifted in art, yet she feels constricted in her small town with its small-town values. Her parents go to church and are quite conservative. Jenny is dating Thomas, who is the clean-cut captain of the football team and son of the richest family in town. Jenny's parents are hoping she will forget her pipe dream of art and instead study law and marry hometown hero Thomas. But Jenny's ex-hippie art teacher, Margaret, believes in Jenny and her gift. She tells her not to give up on her dream like she did and encourages her to study art in Florence, Italy.

Much to the chagrin of her parents, Jenny leaves for Italy, where she discovers a vibrant cosmopolitan culture. Jenny's professor pushes her to "free up her art," saying she is too repressed and needs to lose her inhibitions. Jenny struggles at first to do so and feels embarrassed and self-conscious—that is, until she begins an affair with the mysterious and handsome Fabrizio. Fabrizio encourages Jenny to push her boundaries and do things she has never done before. They smoke a joint, steal a watch for the fun of it, and make passionate, uninhibited love. Jenny has changed: her once tied-up hair now is worn loose, and her conservative clothes have been replaced by colorful dresses. She is no longer the repressed small-town girl but rather a sensual and cosmopolitan woman. Jenny is finally happy.

Everything is going wonderfully until her parents turn up on her doorstep with Thomas. They deliver an ultimatum: either she returns home and marries Thomas, or they will no longer continue to fund her time in Florence. Unwilling to disappoint her family and friends, she agrees to marry Thomas, but just as the minister is about to conduct the ceremony, the unshaven, long-haired Fabrizio appears in the church doorway, singing a song he has written for Jenny. Her mother, with a tear in her eye, tells her to go with Fabrizio because she also once gave up on her true love. The final scene shows Jenny riding off into the sunset on the back of Fabrizio's motorbike.

The values of this made-up film echo the values of the follow-your-desires life script; we are told that the rules of society are stifling, that people follow them because they are repressed, and that to find happiness you must follow your desires and act on them. I'm sure you could list dozens of movies that mirror these scripts; they are the two competing messages our culture gives us. There is no clear solution for reconciling them; thus, we find ourselves directionless and torn. We are searching for our true selves without a compass.

Living between these two tensions leads to intense personal

stress; it can also lead to anxiety, depression, and guilt. Since our culture offers no help for resolving this issue, we create valves to relieve some of the pressure. The office worker starts listening to punk; the housewife gets a tattoo; the senior citizen buys a motorbike. An entire industry is devoted to creating opportunities for people to ease the tension of living between the rules and our desires.

TORN APART

The great African theologian Augustine of Hippo well knew this tension between the rules and our desires. Written between AD 397 and 398, his famous book *Confessions* charts his attempts to grow spiritually by wrestling with his very human desires. Augustine became a Christian at a very young age, although he later walked away from his faith. He lived between two extremes for a time, and finally he simply gave in to his temptations, letting his desires take over his whole life. He began a long-term sexual relationship with a woman who was not his wife. He also became addicted to the murderous, violent entertainments of bloodlust in the Roman Colosseum.

In an effort to rid himself of these desires, he became part of a highly ordered philosophy of the Manichee religion. Basically the Manichees were a sort of Christian cult whose behavior would make Ned Flanders look like Hugh Hefner: they were incredibly fastidious in their attempts to flee what they saw as the evil of the material world. Their rules were extremely difficult to follow and included prohibitions against everything from having sex to plucking fruit. Naturally, life as a Manichee was very difficult; therefore, they would employ people whom they viewed as inferior to do their daily work and chores. In this way the Manichees avoided being contaminated by the world.

Augustine was caught between two visions of life: one that encouraged complete abandon to the desire for gratification and another that shunned human desires altogether. Understanding this, we can relate to his frustration as he writes, "So these two wills within me, one old, one new, one the servant of flesh, the other of the spirit, were in conflict and between them they tore my soul apart."[11] In many ways, Augustine's sentiment echoes the struggles of many of the Christian young adults I meet. They are caught between two models of dealing with desire that do little to move them toward a working spirituality and a true sense of self. However, the Bible offers a completely different approach: the redemption of our desires.

BREAKING IN THE WILD STALLION

Jewish spirituality has much to offer at this point, giving us a way of dealing with our desires that is both biblical and practical. I believe that Jewish spirituality has retained the holistic view of life and faith that we find in both the Old and New Testaments. It has a unique way of looking at our desires, wills, and egos. Rabbi Harold Kushner wrote:

> We dream of leaving the world a better place for our having passed through it, though we often wonder whether, in our quest for significance, we litter the world with our mistakes more than we bless it with our accomplishments. Our souls are split, part of us reaching for goodness, part of us chasing fame and fortune and doing questionable things along the way, as we realize that those two paths may diverge sharply. Our self-image is like an out-of-focus photograph, two slightly blurred images instead of one clear one.[12]

Jewish spirituality teaches us that, on one hand, we have in us the potential to do enormous good—to help others, to make the world a better place, and to move in harmony with God as he re-creates the world. This is the good impulse within us, or, in Hebrew, the Yetzer Ha'tov. Yet at the same time, we also have within us the potential to hurt others, to say unkind things, to be indifferent and insecure, to be selfish and self-destructive, and to resist what God is doing in the world. This is the bad or evil impulse, or the Yetzer Ha'ra.

The Yetzer Ha'ra acts as a kind of inner adversary, presenting us with challenges, temptations, and off-ramps every time we attempt to move in synergy with God. The fascinating thing is that the collection of Jewish rabbinical wisdom known as the Talmud says, "The greater a person the greater their Yetzer Ha'ra." This might help to explain why so many leaders have great falls from grace. As I've spent time with many key Christian leaders, I've noticed that almost all of them have struggled with great personal demons—depression, substance abuse, and sexual brokenness, to name a few. Moreover, as I've read the biographies of great Christian thinkers and theologians, I've learned that many of them have wrestled with seasons of doubt and barrenness.

This applies to others who have made great contributions to our culture. Think of the great artists who struggle with mental health issues, their creativity taking them sometimes to the edge of insanity; the groundbreaking musicians who wrestle daily with insecurity and the fear of how others will receive their work; the world-famous comedians who battle depression and bipolar disorder. Our impact seems to be directly connected to our ability to struggle with those dark impulses inside of us, hell-bent on destroying us.

NOT THE EVIL IN US BUT THE IMPULSE TO DO EVIL

It is key to point out that the rabbis describe the Yetzer Ha'ra as "not the evil in us but the impulse to do evil," or the temptation to become slaves to our lower impulses. These impulses represent some of our most basic needs: the desire for sex, for food, for companionship, for achievement. However, when these impulses lose their divinely ordained place in the order of creation, they can become evil. For example, unlike some other religions that view sex as unholy, the Bible determines the holiness of sex by the intent behind it. Jewish writer George Robinson wrote, "In sex, the yetzer hara takes the form of what we know as the libido. . . . Clearly, the yetzer hara, as it manifests itself in sexuality, is a source of powerful energy and drives, many of them creative (and procreative)."[13] When put in their proper place under God's sovereignty, our impulses and desires can be powerful tools; yet out of balance, they can lead to destruction. Sex can be an uncaring and empty act between two self-loathing individuals, or it can be the pinnacle of a lifelong commitment that becomes a spiritual act of worship. Food can be used for gluttony or for spiritual celebration. The drive in humans to build, create, and achieve can bring blessings, but it also can lead to workaholism. Even ministry can turn from a partnership with God to an act of power-mongering and self-interest. Our desires are not evil in themselves; rather, the way they are directed is what makes them evil or holy.

To illustrate this point, the rabbis tell a fable in which they capture humanity's Yetzer Ha'ra in a pot and attempt to destroy it. However, the next day the people don't go to work, and even the chickens stop laying eggs. The point is that God has placed our human desires in us for a purpose; they are not to be destroyed but harnessed. Speaking of the Rabbi's many references to the Yetzer Ha'ra, Jewish writer Alan Morinis explains:

> These references tell us that despite the literal translation of its name, the yetzer ha'ra isn't an impulse to do harm that dooms us all. Rather, they are pointing to the inner drives that arise

from our lower selves. The drives themselves are certainly not appraised as bad; in fact, they are necessary and useful for human life. But whenever you try to control or overrule those drives because of an intention of your higher nature, or when one of those drives becomes exaggerated, you will have a struggle on your hands. The yetzer ha'ra will do everything in its power to subvert your higher self and to influence you and to indulge your desires. Hence the goal is not to try to destroy the yetzer ha'ra but to control it and apply it for good.[14]

I've heard several rabbis, in order to explain the concept of Yetzer Ha'ra, use the example of an old *Star Trek* episode. In the episode, Captain Kirk, while being transported, is split into two identical versions of himself, except that one is good and one is evil. At first it seems like an easy problem to solve: the Kirk that survives surely must be the good one. But the good Kirk is totally unable to fight against the bad Kirk: he is passive and indecisive; he flip-flops and fears making the wrong decision. While he would like to make good things happen, he has no way of doing so.

I have seen some Christians become Good Kirks. They fall into the trap of letting others walk all over them, all the while feeling religiously justified. They become doormats and martyrs. They constantly put themselves down. They prefer to be "nice" rather than do what God is calling them to do. They choose the path of placation instead of prophecy. Often these people fail to challenge themselves or those around them to grow. It is only when the two Kirks are reunited that the captain is again able to lead his crew. In its proper place, Kirk's dark side is redeemed; properly balanced, it doesn't cause evil but rather provides him with the guile and impetus he needs as a leader. The real Kirk was not Kirk minus his dark side; it was Kirk with his dark side redeemed.

HOLY PARADOX

This kind of paradox may initially seem strange to us, but if you look at Christianity, you'll find that it's filled with paradoxical truths. Because our Western culture is built on a philosophical foundation that is uncomfortable with paradox and mystery, the idea of seemingly contradictory truths can be confusing. But if you think about it, much of our faith is based on paradoxes. For example, God is totally in control of his creation, not letting a sparrow fall from the sky apart from his will, yet he also allows us to have free choice. How on earth does this work?

God is also a God of justice: he calls us to account for the wrong that we do. Like a father, he pushes us to do better and points out when we have not lived up to his expectations. Yet at the same time, God is a God of love. He is filled with grace, showing mercy to those who have done wrong. Like a mother, he will always be ready to take us back no matter what we have done wrong.

Furthermore, God is an unknowable, transcendent God, the Creator of distant constellations that we will never see. His power is beyond our imagination. Yet at the same time, he is our friend. He is close; we can call on him.

Christianity is filled with so many paradoxical truths that some use this as a reason not to believe. Islam points the finger at Christianity, calling Christians unreasonable and rejecting our belief that Jesus can be both fully human and fully divine. When we grapple with such paradoxical truths, we find ourselves seeking balance. We're entering the wonderful place of creative tension. By holding two seemingly contradictory truths next to each other, we find that they point beyond themselves to a greater truth. We are forced to accept the limitations of our human knowledge, to come to the humbling conclusion that, unlike God, we are part of creation and will not come to complete understanding this side of the resurrection of the believers.

DESIRE, THE ENGINE ROOM OF THE SOUL

Our desires act as engine rooms for spiritual growth. They have the potential to move us toward our true selves or away from them. Jesus tells his disciples, "What comes out of you is what defiles you. For from within, out of your hearts, come evil thoughts, sexual immorality, theft, murder, adultery, greed, malice, deceit, lewdness, envy, slander, arrogance and folly. All these evils come from inside and defile you" (Mark 7:20–23). Note his use of the word *heart*; we often use this word in Christian culture without really thinking about what we are saying. We say, "Jesus came into my heart," or "I felt it in my heart," but when Jesus used the word *heart*, he was speaking of that deep hidden place within us, that place where our desires, wills, and egos reside.

Note also in this passage how Jesus labels the ways in which our hearts can be defiled. Reading this passage through twenty-first-century eyes, we can easily pin Jesus down as a stodgy moralist. But Jesus is not just picking on human behavior; he is speaking of how, in our hearts, we can allow our desires and attitudes to become exaggerated and infected.

Looking at the opposites of the sins Jesus mentions is an interesting exercise:

Evil thoughts	→	Peace of mind
Sexual immorality	→	Sexual fulfillment
Theft	→	Giving
Murder	→	Giving others life
Envy	→	Championing others

Arrogance	→	True sense of self
Greed	→	Generosity
Malice	→	Compassion
Deceit	→	Honesty
Lewdness	→	Humanizing
Slander	→	Encouragement
Folly	→	Wisdom

Imagine for a second that you were able to truthfully say the following about yourself: "I have balance within myself. I have found my true identity and now feel peace of mind. I have a true sense of my self-worth. I enjoy sexual fulfillment. I find myself making life decisions that are wise and rewarding. I encourage others and find joy in their triumphs. Others would describe me as compassionate, life-giving, generous, and honest."

Now let's take it further. Imagine if everyone in your town or city could say these things about their lives. Wouldn't that be an amazing place to live? Imagine a town where no one was jealous, angry, sexually broken, arrogant, unwise, violent, or greedy. But take it even further. Imagine living on planet Earth with all people able to say the same of their lives. Would there be war, hunger, corruption, or crime? Call me naive, but I don't think there would be. Hopefully by now you see the genius of Jesus at work. He attacks the core issues in the human heart, pointing out that when our desires are out of order, when our egos are wounded, when we look for a sense of power and control apart from God, there are consequences, not just for us, but for our families, cities, cultures, nations, and the whole of creation. Jesus makes clear that the redemption of our desires is key; it is the beginning point of the redemption of the world. We must change and move toward our true selves. This, however, is a lot easier said than done.

WHEN YOUR GUARD IS DOWN

The political humorist P. J. O'Rourke once said, "Everybody wants to save the earth; nobody wants to help Mom do the dishes."[15] O'Rourke is observing that everyone desires grand change in our world, yet we so often resist change when it affects us. We are happy for someone to rid the world of apathy, but we are often not so keen to rid ourselves of apathy. Most of the time we desire for ourselves to change and be redeemed by Christ, but sometimes we resist that change. Paul, with his knowledge of the Torah, understood that our desires have the greatest potential to derail us when our guard is down; that's why he encouraged the communities to whom he wrote to live holy lives.

We all know it's easier to be holy in certain circumstances than in others. Ironically, we often treat people we don't know better than those we love. It's easy to be ethical or to act holy when we are on display, but when we are run down, tired, and alone, we find ourselves giving in to temptation. Studies have shown that many ministers who fall morally do so on Mondays; it's easy to be holy in front of the congregation midsermon, but once the adulation and adrenaline are gone, many ministers act less than holy. As a minister, I've seen couples fall into this trap again and again. While they are dating, they dote on each other and treat each other with respect in an attempt to win each other over, but as soon as the honeymoon ends and the ordinary domestic life of marriage begins, many couples start taking each other for granted, often mimicking the very behaviors for which they criticize their parents. The guy who was determined not to be as distant, cold, and uncaring as his father wakes up at age thirty-eight to find that, despite his best efforts, he has become just like his father. It is in these moments when our unredeemed wills are exposed, when our desires continue to slowly move away from

God's ordained order, and when our egos are wounded that evil enters the picture.

EVIL AND THE UNREDEEMED SELF

Our culture loves to neatly package people into two camps—those who do evil and those who do good. But biblical spirituality is far subtler; it doesn't offer such a simplistic answer. The Bible claims that all of us are capable of evil acts.

In the countryside of Cambodia, there stands a tree with a large crater in its side. The tree has this hole in it because thousands of babies' skulls were smashed against it for days on end during a massacre of people who were chosen by Pol Pot's regime to be killed. A Cambodian Christian who lived during the time of the killing fields described the terror of the Khmer Rouges' murderous government as "hell coming to earth." What is particularly tragic about the horror that occurred in Cambodia, in which an estimated two million Cambodians were killed, is that it wasn't carried out by one people group against another. It involved an entire culture, a whole nation turned upon itself.

The killing fields of Cambodia, the millions killed by Stalin, and the Nazi concentration camps are all testaments to how far humans can follow their evil desires. If you think about it, the most evil events in the history of humanity have been brought about by humans. For evil to happen, human hands are needed. Our unredeemed selves, our wounded egos, and our basest desires are the fuel for the fire of evil. Our image-driven culture, which ignores the inner self, has very little chance of changing our world. Our world has more than enough food to feed everyone and plenty of resources to put an end to poverty, yet we are locked in a cycle of poverty, corruption, violence, and war because of the human heart's self-interest. Sadly, most people desire for the world to be as it is supposed to be, but through our unredeemed wills, we find ourselves compromising that goal. While our reluctance to move toward our true selves results in pain for ourselves, our active resistance to our God-given identity creates the environment for evil to take hold. Psychiatrist M. Scott Peck rightly points out that it is our resistance to spiritual growth that creates the conditions for evil to flourish:

> Truly evil people . . . actively rather than passively avoid extending themselves. They will take any action in their power to protect their own laziness, to preserve their sick self. Rather than nurturing others they will actually destroy others in this cause. . . . I define evil, then, as the . . . imposition of one's will upon others by overt or covert coercion—in order to avoid extending one's self for the purpose of nurturing spiritual growth.[16]

We are called to join God in the fight against evil in the world; however, the twist in the plot is that part of this resistance to evil entails a fight against the evil (or the potential for evil) that we find in our own hearts. Thus, we must take seriously the way that our wills and desires can sabotage us. The road away from our true selves is the slippery slope to evil.

When Paul in his letter to Timothy wrote that leaders in the church should be faithful in their marriages, not given to drunkenness, not lovers of money, gentle, well regarded, and not conceited,[17] he was not setting out a test to ensure that the church is filled with "holy Joes"; rather, he was laying out an incredible framework with which to redeem the world. He was not just picking on various behaviors; he was outlining the ways that certain behaviors indicate the state of our hearts. These behaviors act as diagnostic tools that reveal the ways in which all is not well with our souls.

Paul understood that these areas are the key battlegrounds in which we, with the Holy Spirit's help, struggle toward becoming our true selves. These are the areas that carry the greatest potential for slip-ups. To begin the journey to becoming our real selves, we must understand ourselves now. We must see how our weaknesses offer us a challenge to move forward. There are few more powerful witnesses than believers who declare war on those parts of themselves that are yet to be redeemed.

WALKING THROUGH LIFE DEAD

To take our flaws seriously, we must approach life as a work of art. To ignore the challenge to grow spiritually or to fail to move toward our true selves is simply to walk through life dead.

Late one night as I rocked my crying baby to sleep, I caught the first part of the British comedy movie *Shaun of the Dead*. The movie pokes fun at the genre of zombie films. The hero is Shaun, an ordinary guy who is so caught up in the minutia of his life that he is unaware that London is being overrun with zombies. In the background a TV blares the news that the apocalypse has come, explosions and sirens can be heard in the distance, and friends and family are turned into zombies—yet Shaun and his friend remain totally distracted. In one scene Shaun walks to a local shop; his head is down and he is caught up thinking about his dysfunctional relationship with his girlfriend. The street is filled with dead bodies, burned-out cars, and people escaping the city, and his neighbors and friends have been turned into the living undead. The humor of the scene is based in the fact that Shaun is so self-obsessed that he fails to notice that anything is wrong. By the time Shaun realizes what is going on, an army of zombies has taken over the city.

As I watched, I couldn't help but think how so many people

I encounter are like Shaun: we major on the minors. We walk through life with our heads down, gazing at the sidewalk, caught up in details that barely matter. All the while the monsters in us and in those around us lay siege to our lives and communities, wreaking their havoc. However, those of us who are determined to take seriously the challenge of spiritual growth see our desires as a chance to find our true selves.

SPIRITUAL JUDO

Biblical spirituality recognizes that our temptations are unique to our personalities. For example, some of us are able to drink alcohol with no ill effects, while others of us find that alcohol harms our health, impedes our ability to make wise decisions, and affects the way we treat others. Some people have no problem enjoying healthy friendships with people of the opposite sex, but for others, the world of relationships is a minefield of sexual and emotional entanglements. Some relationships, no matter how innocent, carry the potential for great destruction. Some people find marriage an oasis of refreshment and joy, while others find it a constant challenge. And some find that having a public profile is simply a by-product of their work, while others find it to be a continual temptation that moves them toward self-obsession and vanity.

Alan Morinis wrote:

> In our uniqueness, you and I have desires that have their own distinctive weave and coloration. And your yetzer ha'ra is matched up to your desires, inch for inch, stitch for stitch. Your yetzer ha'ra is perfectly contoured to provide exactly the challenges you must overcome in order to grow spiritually. And just as there is an infinite range of human personalities, the yetzer

ha'ra comes in an infinite number of variations. In every case, though, the yetzer ha'ra will perfectly match a person's spiritual curriculum. . . . You are well advised to get to know yours.[18]

When I first read Morinis's statement, I thought surely things don't fit that snugly; surely the temptations we face aren't always in the areas in which we are meant to grow at that time. But I have to admit that as I've reflected on my pastoral experience, and as I think of the hundreds of people whose lives I've had the privilege to peer into, I've seen repeatedly that they are presented with the same challenges. Many fall again and again at the same hurdle. Over decades the same issue or temptation keeps cropping up, albeit in different garb. Others will conquer a particular challenge only to be presented with new challenges for a new season. I have come to agree with Morinis's statement that we are challenged and tempted in the areas in which we are meant to grow. While we can't avoid challenges and temptations, we can choose how we respond to them when they arise.

MOVING TOWARD PEACE

To redeem our wills, egos, and desires, to move toward our true selves, we must understand the power of peace. As we have established, God calls us to holiness. Holiness is a state of wholeness. Jesus says in John's gospel that the gift he brings to the world is the gift of peace, a peace that is unlike the peace the world offers (see John 14:27). The English word *peace* doesn't fully capture what Jesus was getting at. Too often when we read the word *peace* in the Bible, we think of the absence of war or the clichéd concept of *peace* peddled by spas and massage centers. But when Jesus spoke of *shalom*, the word held a whole wealth of meaning for his Jewish listeners.[19] *Shalom* means wholeness, balance, well-being, safety, and prosperity. It is everything in its right place—life exactly as God planned it, life without the effects of sin, evil, and death. Many Christian writers of late have explored the social, political, and economic dimensions of the concept of shalom, yet not many have explored what shalom means for the individual. The reach of God's dream of shalom moves from the whole of creation all the way down to us as individuals. It is us as we were originally meant to be—whole, balanced, safe in the perfect will of God.

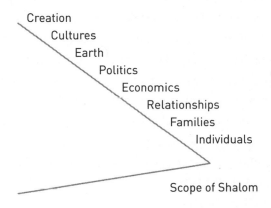

Creation
Cultures
Earth
Politics
Economics
Relationships
Families
Individuals

Scope of Shalom

In his letter to the Philippians, Paul wrote, "Do not be anxious about anything, but in every situation, by prayer and petition, with thanksgiving, present your requests to God. And the peace of God, which transcends all understanding, will guard your hearts and your minds in Christ Jesus" (Phil. 4:6–7). Paul was describing holy peace, a divine gift of shalom that is greater and more wonderful than the human mind can understand. When we follow Christ, Paul says, this shalom peace, this heavenly wholeness, will guard our hearts and minds. In the previous verse, Paul tells the believers not to worry, thus setting up a contrast between those who anxiously attempt to gain a sense of control over their world and those who put their trust in God. Those who hand over their whole lives to God can actually begin to experience shalom here in this life.

RULING OVER SIN

The story of Cain and Abel is one of the first stories we encounter in the Bible. It is also one of the most tragic. Cain and Abel were the children of Adam and Eve, and they both paid a heavy price as sin entered the world and began its battle with the human condition. Both brothers offered God the fruits of their labor, but while Abel offered God his best, Cain's offering was paltry and begrudgingly given. Thus, God's favor fell on Abel rather than Cain.

Cain's ego was wounded, and jealousy began to well up in him. Eventually this jealousy overwhelmed Cain, and he murdered his brother. His punishment was banishment from the land. For a nomadic person, this sentence was almost worse than death. Marked by God, he was unable to be killed. His punishment is summed up in a seemingly trivial (but upon closer examination, tragic) verse that reads, "So Cain went out from the LORD's presence and lived in the land of Nod, east of Eden" (Gen. 4:16).

Cain's parents began life happily in the perfect environment in which God dwelled among them, but they were sent out from that place. Cain continued his parents' journey away from God's presence—he was even further away from humanity's original home of Eden. French sociologist and theologian Jacques Ellul comments that geographers know of no land of Nod. After reading the sentence in Genesis in which Cain goes out from the Lord's presence and lives East of Eden he observed:

> When I first read it, that sentence set me to dreaming. Unknown to geographers! And what kind of land would it be, this Nowhere land, which is not a place but a lack of place, the opposite of Eden . . . The seed of all man's questing is to be found in Cain's life in the land of wandering, always searching for a place where his need for security might be satisfied. But

the only place he finds is that very country characterized by being uninhabitable.[20]

Cain here is a cautionary figure. He has let his human emotions overrun him and therefore finds himself always outside of God's presence. Eden is always in the distance as a reminder of what he and his family have lost. He will always search, always want more. His deepest desires will never be satisfied. Ellul notes that it was Cain who built the first city. In an attempt to go it alone, he tried to create a human alternative to the reign of God. He placed the first brick in the foundation of what would be symbolized by Babel, Babylon, Rome, and our twenty-first-century global culture. Cain's tragic memory looms large over our culture and our understanding of self as we continually seek more, looking for our deepest needs to be met in the wrong places. However, if we delve back into the story, we find an element that many miss in the tragic account of Cain. After Cain has given his less-than-impressive offering, God says to him, "Why are you angry? Why is your face downcast? If you do what is right, will you not be accepted? But if you do not do what is right, sin is crouching at your door; it desires to have you, but you must rule over it" (Gen. 4:6–7).

God first notes that anger is growing in Cain. If he does what is right, he will be accepted by God. But if he lets this anger grow into sin, like a monster it will take him over—he will become his anger. God is offering Cain the chance to confess his anger, to bring it into divine light. Fascinatingly, God advises Cain that he must rule over his sin. He must command it, not let it grow into an uncontrollable and destructive beast. God is telling him to put anger in its proper place.

It's natural to instinctively feel angry and slighted sometimes, but it's what we do next that counts. Think now about what would have happened if Cain hadn't let his anger grow, if he had followed

God's advice to master his emotions lest they develop into sin and death. Note God's tone: it is questioning and conversational. His words don't sound like commandments; they sound like wise counsel. God humanizes Cain by allowing him free choice, just as he had given Cain's parents free choice in the garden. God is teaching Cain, and us, a basic principle—allow your desires to grow out of control, and you will always live with those desires unfulfilled, trying to make them happen on your own rather than relying on God's providence. You will find yourself living "east of Eden," in an uninhabitable land where there is no satisfaction, while your true self remains distant and cloudy.

SOUL FRIENDS

Including others in our quest for spiritual balance is important. The ancient Christian Celts of Britain practiced a spiritual discipline known as *Anam Cara*, or "Soul Friends." The Soul Friend's job was to act as a spiritual companion along the path of holiness. These individuals would point out blind spots and hear confessions, but perhaps most interesting to us, they would offer what was known as "remedies of the soul's disease." Vices or sin would be healed by the opposite of that vice. The seventh-century Christian Celtic writer Cummean wrote, "The eight principal vices . . . shall be healed by the eight remedies that are their contraries."[21] (The Celts saw these eight principal vices to be gluttony, sexual sin, greed, anger, self-pity, laziness, vanity, and pride.) This ancient but brilliant strategy allows unredeemed desires within us to return to a state of balance.

A believer, with the help of a Soul Friend, would identify an area in which a vice was taking control. They would devise a practical task to undertake in order to rectify or "make right" that sin, thus moving toward wholeness. Ray Simpson, who is both a historian of Celtic Christianity and the leader of a modern-day Celtic Christian community, notes that while members of the Catholic Church on the European continent would go to a priest to confess their sins, the Celtic Christians would enact a form of penance or restitution in order to make right what had been made wrong with the individual they had wronged rather than confessing to a priest. Through restitution, or the mending of that which was broken, things were moved toward a state of shalom.[22] What's fascinating is that this practice recognized the way in which sin diminished the whole community. Thus, restitution had the potential to transform not only the individual but the whole community. As Ray Simpson wrote:

> We learn from Columbanus' Rule that if someone stole something from their neighbor, then they had to restore it. If they had stolen so many things over too long a period to be able to pay them all back, then they had to live on bread and water for a specified period and give a proportion of income from their work for the relief of the poor. These are principles which, if they were applied regardless of whether they were cost-effective, could transform our society as much as Celtic Society.[23]

We can see this spirit of balance and transformation at work in the life of Levi, the tax collector (Luke 5:27–32). Levi collaborated with the oppressing Roman army; he profited financially from the suffering of his own people and nation. He was so obsessed with personal gain that he allowed himself to be ruled by greed and turned his back on his people in their hour of need. After World War II, intense anger was poured out on those who had turned their backs on their own people and collaborated with the Nazis for personal gain; they were shunned, publicly humiliated, and even tortured to death for their acts of treachery. This is the anger that Levi's friends, family, and neighbors would have felt toward him. Yet after his encounter with Jesus, he was no longer acting selfishly or making a lonely fortune. He was no longer divorced from his community; he had been transformed with the spirit of generosity, and so he threw a party, a feast. His soul was balanced. He was at one with God, himself, and his community. Shalom came in the form of his party.

THE TEMPTATION OF IMBALANCE

We must remember that as we move toward an internal shalom balance, we will find the evil one pushing us toward any form of imbalance. We may avoid one extreme form of desire only to exchange it for another. This kind of trade-off is a classic mistake that has been made throughout Christian history.

There is a wise story about the chief rabbi of England being called to give evidence at a trial. His lawyer asks him whether it is true that he is the greatest expert on Jewish law in all of Europe. He replies that he is. At this point the judge interjects, asking him whether that is an arrogant opinion for a supposed holy man to hold, to which the rabbi replies, "What can I do? I am under oath."[24]

The rabbi's point is a valid one. He, in his honest assessment, was regarded by his community and peers to be the finest expert on Jewish law in Europe. To feign humility and pretend that he wasn't would be to go to another extreme, the polar opposite of arrogance, self-hatred as the antidote to arrogance. Such a view of himself would have been just as unbalanced, just as much a denial of his God-given identity as unjustified pride would have been. By taking things to the opposite extreme, we walk off the road of holiness and into legalism and holier-than-thou piety. We make the mistake of the early church theologian Origen, who was so disturbed by his struggles with sexual desires that he cut off his own genitals. His genitals were never the problem; in fact, they had been given to him as a gift from his Maker, if only he had learned to redeem the monster of lust. Origen's desire to fight lust and transform himself into the image of God actually led him to mutilate God's good creation. The key is to find the middle ground, the balancing point, the perfection of God's shalom.

PUTTING DESIRE IN ITS SHALOM PLACE

Desire is a powerful force. The good things of this world require shalom and balance; they require an internal return to equilibrium, which in turn brings peace to ourselves. Our desires are tools with tremendous potential for sustaining us and equal potential for destroying us. A chainsaw in the hands of an ice sculptor can lead to beauty; a chainsaw in the hands of a child can lead to tragedy. The great Christian writer C. S. Lewis claimed that Christians have too limited a view of desire:

> Indeed, if we consider the unblushing promises of reward and the staggering nature of the rewards promised in the Gospel, it would seem that Our Lord finds our desires, not too strong, but too weak. We are half-hearted creatures, fooling about with drink and sex and ambition when infinite joy is offered us, like an ignorant child who wants to go on making mud pies in a slum because he cannot imagine what is meant by the offer of a holiday to the sea. We are too easily pleased.[25]

Lewis explains that the deep desires we feel within us point to a greater reality; therefore, they must be pointed toward God. Imagine a woman living alone in a large and lonely city. Each day she wakes up and goes through the same routine of commuting to work, working, and returning home. Several years earlier, she had given up on ever meeting a soul mate; however, every time she opens the door at the end of the day to enter her apartment, she can't help but imagine what it would be like to come home, not to an empty space, but to a loving husband.

One day she comes home and finds a parcel on her doorstep; in the parcel she finds a dress. Confused, she looks to see if there is a return address, but there is nothing except her name and address written in clear handwriting. The woman lifts the dress from the package, and for a second she finds her breath taken away. She has never seen anything so beautiful, even in the most expensive shops. Its colors match the natural tones of her skin and hair. The stitching and detailing are immaculate. The fabric's softness and lightness are almost otherworldly. Cautiously she holds the dress up against herself—it seems to be the right size. With a mixture of curiosity and excitement, she finds herself skipping across the apartment into her bedroom to try on the dress. To her great surprise, the dress fits perfectly. It is as if it has been precisely tailored for her by the finest of dressmakers. She can barely look up at her full-length mirror, but as she does, she can't believe what she sees. The cut, the colors, and the fabric all conspire to take years and pounds off her in a way that no other dress could. She sees in the mirror a smile breaking out across her face, the kind of smile she has not experienced since she was a teenager, when the adventure and mystery of life seemed to stretch out before her. Then out of the corner of her eye she sees it. In the excitement of trying on the dress, she didn't notice it drop. A small note the size of a business card has fallen out of the package and lies on the carpet in her bedroom doorway. Almost shaking, the woman picks up the card. It simply reads, "I had this dress made for you because I see a beauty and grace in you that the world misses. Love, your secret admirer."

This woman has two ways of processing what has just

happened. The first option is to forget about who gave her the dress and just be happy that she scored a free dress. She can wear it to the office Christmas party and thank her lucky stars. The second option is to wonder and dream about who her mystery admirer could be. She could ask herself, *Who would go to such lengths to do this for me? Who could know me so well as to have been able to make the perfect dress for me?* She could look at the dress as an object in and of itself, or she could look at the dress and see that it points beyond itself to the dress-giver. She could look at the dress and see what it tells her about the person who gave it to her.

Christian writer Philip Yancey wrote:

> I realized that natural desire was not an enemy of the supernatural and repressing desire not the solution. Rather, to find the path of joy I needed to connect desire to its otherworldly source. . . . My natural desires, I now see, are pointers to the supernatural, not obstacles. In a world fallen far from its original design, God wants us to receive them as gifts and not possessions, tokens of love and not loves in themselves.[26]

God wants us to appreciate his gifts to us. Our humanity and the desires of humanity are his gifts to us. Our drives to procreate, to enjoy, and to feel excitement and joy are just a few of the blessings he bestows upon his children. However, too often we become lazy. We choose not to look beyond the gifts we are given; instead, we attempt, as Yancey says, to turn these gifts into possessions. We worship the gift, not the Giver of gifts.

FOUR KEYS TO BALANCE

Scripture provides us with four great themes that aid us as we attempt to bring balance to our impulses and desires. They help us to redeem our desires so that we can move toward our future selves.

1. Bringing Our Desires Under Christ's Lordship

The place to begin is with a thorough self-evaluation that brings to light the ways our desires have spun out of control. Many of us already know deep down the areas in which we fail to live up to God's best for our lives. However, the ways in which we need to change often hide in the darkness. And like mushrooms, our unredeemed desires grow best in the darkness. But if we are to bring shalom, balance, and wholeness to these areas, we must connect them to the source of shalom, God. Through prayer and confession, we must bring before him the ways in which we walk away from our true selves. By doing so, we create a space in which to begin our transformation into the people we are meant to be.

If our unredeemed desires grow best in the deep, dark places within us, the soil in which spiritual growth begins is the soil of humility. Humility is a forgotten art in our culture of self-promotion and self-obsession. By admitting that we are works in progress, by admitting that we don't have it all together, we create a space of humility. We are saying that when it comes to becoming fully human, we don't have all the answers; those answers are to be found only in God. Only when our hearts are humble can we begin to move forward.

2. Bringing Our Desires Under Covenant

The concept of covenant runs throughout the Bible. God's preferential state of relationship is covenant, a state of utmost commitment, unconditional love, and great risk. Marriage is one of the only echoes of covenantal relationship in our culture. It is a relationship in which the commitment is kept even though better options may come along. It is a full-blooded, wholehearted commitment. When Christ returns, the world will exist in covenantal relationship. The Bible calls us to covenantal relationship with other believers, with the poor (Proverbs 31:20), with the marginalized and despised (Luke 10:25–37), with creation (Genesis 1:28–31), and even with our enemies (Luke 6:35). Therefore, we must ensure that our desires move us toward covenantal relationship. By doing so, we undermine the strain of radical individualism that has so subverted faith in the West. We must ask ourselves, "Is this desire moving me toward greater commitment or away from it?"

3. Testing the Worthiness of Our Desires

The Bible speaks of our bodies as temples in which the Spirit dwells. It speaks of our whole selves as being created in the image of God. Thus, a great way to test the worthiness of our desires is to examine whether they reflect a respect of the image of God in others and ourselves. Our culture has moved away from the idea of respecting the image of God in others. Instead, it turns others into mere social images and robs them of their humanity. Cultural critic Donald Richie observes:

> We live in such an inundating sea of images that it is a commonplace that we now look at the image and not at the thing itself. . . . A result is that essence is turned into surface and integrity vanishes. . . . We have now reached an age where we may be beginning to appreciate the biblical second commandment which, as you will remember, says that: "Thou shalt not make unto thee any graven image, any likeness of any thing."[27]

This modern form of image-driven idolatry permeates our lives. Pornography turns people into mere images; the public relations spin on war turns civilian casualties into collateral damage;

the news reports victims of starvation as mere statistics; our workplaces turn our coworkers into competitors; the mentally ill and homeless become an urban nuisance. In the contemporary climate, even our friends, spouses, and families can be reduced to annoyances, obstacles in our quest to get what we want out of life. Thus, we end up denying the image of God in them.

Our culture of excess and addiction can diminish our God-given identity. Our bodies and minds often act as early warning systems. Overconsumption of junk food, workaholism, alcohol and drug abuse, stress, anger, and hatred are all scientifically proven to eat away at God's gift of our health and our bodies. Therefore, we must ask ourselves whether our desires are helping us cultivate the image of God in us. Scripture is the standard against which we can hold up our desires to ensure that we are respecting the image of God.

4. Testing the Fruitfulness of Our Desires

We can tell something is in correct balance when it produces fruit. God's coming kingdom of shalom is a place of fruitfulness. Consequently, when our desires are in their proper place, they will contribute to the kingdom—they will make the world a better place. Our desires are put in us to bless us and those around us. God calls us to be holy as he is holy; therefore, just as it is God's nature to give, to cultivate, and to bless, so also should our desires add to the world. An excellent test of our desires and impulses is to ask whether they are cultivating fruit in others. As Paul says in his first letter to the believers in Corinth, "So whether you eat or drink or whatever you do, do it all for the glory of God. Do not cause anyone to stumble" (1 Cor. 10:31–32).

CHAPTER 11

Playing Inside the Piano

When I went to see the brilliantly creative Japanese composer and musician Ryuichi Sakamoto in concert, I found myself rethinking how I viewed my faith. The performance began fairly normally: Sakamoto walked out to the audience's applause, bowed, and then sat down at his piano. He started to play in the conventional manner, sitting on the piano stool and stroking the keys. As the performance continued, however, I was surprised to see Sakamoto rise from his seat, slide forward, lie atop the open grand piano, and begin to play amazing music from inside the piano by hitting the strings inside the instrument. I realized that night that there was more than one way to play a piano.

It is the same with our faith. Most of us think we understand biblical spirituality; we think we have heard it all before. Yet the more I learn, the more I realize that biblical faith is like Sakamoto's piano. Just when you think you understand it, it radically surprises you. The Bible is like a never-ending river of spiritual resources, like one of those computer-generated fractals that keeps going deeper and becoming more vivid. The Bible has radical ways of teaching us about the redemption of our desires and the path toward holiness and shalom. Let's get inside the piano.

REDEEMING OUR DESIRES

One of the exciting things I've realized as a believer is that even the most seemingly unredeemable impulses and desires in humans can be redeemed. Take jealousy. Our culture looks at jealousy as an unfortunate trait that can destroy relationships. It reeks of possessiveness and insecurity. What on earth could be redeemable about jealousy? How could jealousy move us forward spiritually?

Well . . . the book of Exodus tells us that God is a jealous God (see 20:5 and 34:14). I have often read this verse to groups of young adults and then asked them to describe the way this makes them imagine God. Mostly people have in their minds a picture of an angry old man, a dysfunctional and violent father figure who bitterly guards his children. But I then reframe the verse, asking the group to think of God not as an angry, bitter old man, but as a passionate lover who is pursuing a woman, a man so smitten, so in love, that he would go to any length and fight any other suitor in order to win over his love. I ask the group to discuss this way of looking at God's relationship with us. An almost immediate change comes over the group. They begin to see jealousy in a very different light.

HOLY JEALOUSY

The Orthodox rabbi and relationship expert Shmuley Boteach brings a radical approach to jealousy, one that he would argue is thoroughly biblical. Pained by the high divorce rate, Boteach believes that marriage therapists and conventional wisdom have wrongly placed too high a value on trust and familiarity in marriage. Boteach writes:

> Marriages should be based not on trust, but on tension. Not on routine, but on raging emotion. Not on respect, but on jealousy. Not on confidence, but suspicion. Sounds crazy, right? But think of it this way: When you trust that your spouse will never be erotically attracted to a stranger and will never be unfaithful, you start taking him or her for granted. Isn't this really the number-one-killer of marriages? Isn't growing bored and "falling out of love" the most lethal of all marital illnesses? Won't a relationship be doomed if a couple is complacent and smug to the point of not having to work at it anymore?[1]

Boteach argues that modern secular culture has turned marriage into something akin to a brother-sister relationship or a platonic friendship, yet at the same time our culture paints adultery or casual sex with strangers as the highest sexual experience. Boteach (who is totally committed to a conservative biblical view of sexuality, in which sex is appropriate only in a committed married relationship) believes that the Bible calls us to married relationships filled with passionate abandon rather than dull domesticity. People will do anything to win over a potential spouse, but more often than not, once the spouse has been caught, people give up trying, and the marriage is suffocated. Boteach points to the Old Testament practice of *mikveh*, in which a menstruating woman would spend time separated from her husband. This practice has often been wrongly interpreted by Christians as having to do with the supposed uncleanness of women's periods. However, in

Jewish culture and particularly the Orthodox tradition, mikveh is a means of separating husband and wife during her period so that they don't become overly familiar with each other. As a result, their passions and desires are heightened.

Part of the reason our culture erotizes adultery and "the stranger" is that as humans and spiritual beings, we are drawn to the familiar, yet we are also drawn to the mysterious. The period of mikveh separation increases the mystery that married couples feel for each other. Thus, Boteach recommends that jealousy, in its correct place, can breathe new, passionate life into a marriage.

Boteach tells the story of a couple who came to him with marital difficulties. He noticed that the husband took his wife for granted; he didn't even find her remotely attractive. Boteach proposed a radical experiment. He told the wife to dress to the nines, head down to the bar, and sit at a table. Boteach ordered the husband to enter the bar separately and sit away from his wife, watching her. The husband began to notice that men in the bar were sneaking glances at his wife. Some men even made advances toward her. When one man initiated an attempt to seduce her, the husband, enraged with jealousy, rushed across the bar, his heart pounding with passion and anger. He almost got into a fight with the man. Suddenly the husband no longer saw the woman he had become so familiar with; instead, he saw this woman whom other men were trying to seduce. Likewise, the wife no longer saw a man who had become bored with her; now he was a lover, fighting off other men just to have her. The couple, whose sex life had been on the rocks, who had fallen out of love with each other, were so filled with passion that they couldn't even make it home and ended up making love in their car. Even Boteach concedes that this is an extreme example, but the point is made: jealousy, brought under the Lordship of God, that is in its correct place, can be holy.

FROM LUST TO APPRECIATION

Even lust can be put in a proper place where it is transformed into an appreciation of beauty that points to the Creator. There is a wonderful story of the early church bishop of Edessa Nonnus. Nonnus was renowned for his faith and humility. One day, as the church leaders of the city sat enthralled by his teaching, they were interrupted by the sight of the most famous and most beautiful woman of their day passing their church door. She was a well-known actress and was moving through the city in a procession. She was covered in jewels; behind her was a train of young men and women, carrying perfumes and scents. Her body was clothed in the finest of gowns. Her appearance caused an uproar among the assembled leaders, and we read that "when the bishops saw her so shamelessly ride by, bare of head and shoulder and limb, in pomp so splendid, and not so much as a veil upon her head or about her shoulder, they groaned, and in silence turned away their heads as from a great and grievous sin."[2] But as they looked away from the woman, they saw Nonnus, whose response to the woman was quite different: "But the most blessed Nonnus did long and most intently regard her: and after she had passed by still he gazed and still his eyes went after her."[3] Nonnus asked the bishops if they found her appearance pleasing, but they remained silent. Nonnus replied that he indeed did find her appearance pleasing, telling them that she was a vision of the bride for whom Christ died. Her beauty was a pointer to the handiwork of the Creator. He was not moved to lust; instead, he was moved to worship.

Even the Bible holds physical beauty in regard. It speaks positively of attractive physical features, but unlike our culture, which tends to see the superficial as an end in and of itself, the Bible places beauty in its proper place. Song of Songs praises human beauty, yet at the same time the book of Ecclesiastes reminds us that looks are fleeting. Our culture tries to turn the physical into a commodity. Instead of seeing beauty as a fleeting pointer to a reality beyond, lust turns us onto a dead-end street. The antidote to lust is to put beauty in its divinely ordered place, to treat it as a calling card from the redeemed world to come.

A VERY NORMAL YOUNG WOMAN
BECOMES A SAINT

One of my favorite Christian leaders is Teresa of Avila. Teresa lived in Spain during the 1500s, when women had very little say in culture, let alone in the Christian church. Moreover, Teresa was born into a mixed Christian-Jewish family—a huge issue during her day because of the infamous Spanish Inquisition, in which Jewish people were persecuted. Even mixed-race families like Teresa's, who had come to believe in Jesus as Messiah, were still viewed with suspicion by church authorities caught up in the delusional quest to rid Catholic Spain of heretical influences.

What is so endearing about Teresa is the fact that her faith was a constant struggle. Hers was a spirituality forged by trial and torment. She wore her heart on her sleeve and tended to develop crushes on her male spiritual directors, thus having to change directors several times. She wrote to one of them of her affections for him: "Father, . . . the flesh is weak and it has felt this more than I should have wished—in fact a great deal."[4] She was renowned for her beauty and personality and no doubt could have used these features inappropriately. Many secular biographers of Teresa have attempted to portray her as a sexually frustrated nun who poured her desire for connection with a man into her spirituality. They have pointed to the famous statue entitled *The Ecstasy of Saint Theresa* by Giovanni Lorenzo Bernini (which depicts Teresa experiencing spiritual ecstasy), viewing the statue with Freudian eyes and noting that her ecstasy seems more sexual that spiritual. But what these writers fail to see is that Teresa *directed* her desires for intimacy and male companionship into her spiritual life.

Yes, there was an erotic element to Teresa's spirituality, because as a nun (and therefore a single and chaste woman), she had to redeem her sexuality as a single person. Her celibacy became a motivation that spurred her on in her spiritual life. As theologian Rodney Clapp wrote, "Human beings are created and redeemed physically, not merely mentally. And there is a place—a necessary place—for the proper Christian appropriation of the erotic, as . . . the right ordering of bodily desires."[5] To me Teresa is a kind of patron saint of single people who struggle with sexual desire. She reminds us that sexuality is about so much more than just the act of sex; it is about the whole person. We need to learn from the wonderful example of Teresa, who loved beautiful dresses and perfume, who felt attractions to her male spiritual directors and confessed a fondness for gossip, yet who harnessed her desires and shortcomings and became one of the most amazing leaders the church has ever seen.

History remembers Teresa as a woman who had profound charismatic experiences and visions that have ministered to believers for hundreds of years. This woman who struggled so, who lived in a time when, because of her gender and ethnicity, her voice was marginalized, has left us with deeply perceptive and piercing spiritual writings that have guided the spiritual lives of countless people of faith. We need to learn from her struggle with her desires and her dedication to stay on the path of holiness, moving closer and closer to her true self.

The Road to Your True Self

From Public Image to Image of God

We examine and renounce the ways in which we have embraced

false selves. We confess the ways in which we have looked to others for a sense of self rather than to God.

From Death to Life

We examine the ways in which we have embraced the patterns of the flesh or *sarx*. We forsake these destructive patterns, removing "that which is not us" from our lives.

From Me to Soul Friend

We find a Soul Friend who will guide us on our journey toward our true selves, who will ask us the hard questions to ensure our spiritual growth. (Pages 142–43 offer a simple way to do this.)

Jesus as Primary Image

We begin to study and imitate the life of Christ, looking to him as the primary image upon which to model our identities.

Harnessed and Redeemed Desire

We bring our desires and impulses under the redemption of Christ. We put them in their right place with the aid of the Holy Spirit. We use this struggle as a foundry for spiritual growth.

Life as Worship

We live abundantly, enjoying all the good things our Creator has given us. We see that all things point toward the Creator, and we live life as a joyous act of worship.

Embracing Your True Self

For the rest of our lives we will walk forward on the path of holiness toward our true selves, each day focusing on becoming more and more like the people God has designed us to be.

JACOB'S FIGHT FOR PEACE

When we first meet Jacob in the book of Genesis, we find him a flawed character. He is filled with resentment toward his brother's status as firstborn. He is also caught up in a competitive cycle with his brother. In some ways it's easy to understand why Jacob felt insecure; his brother, Esau, was the ultimate macho figure—great at hunting, masculine, and strong. Jacob, in contrast, spent his time with the womenfolk around the campfire. In the ancient culture of the Middle East, you could say that if Esau was the alpha male, Jacob was more like the omega male. We find Jacob unable to assert a sense of personal power. He is easily manipulated by his mother, and he becomes manipulative and duplicitous himself.

Now, you may remember the story of Jacob stealing his brother's firstborn blessing through an act of deceit, but you might not realize that this ancient story carries a powerful message for us today. His story is a great encouragement to those of us living in an age in which we have embraced false selves.

Jacob's father, Isaac, was blind and could only recognize people through touch. Jacob put on an animal's fur, thus imitating the feel of his hairy brother, and pretended to be Esau. He tricked his father into giving him his brother's blessing. In a similar way, many of us today have embraced false selves: we are either too lazy, too afraid, or too insecure to allow others to see us as we really are. Instead, we project a false image in order to gain the blessings and rewards of our culture. (When interpreting this story, Harold Kushner notes that in some ways Jacob is not being manipulative—part of him really wants to be his twin brother. He is looking to others to find the wholeness that he craves.[6]) We choose not to take responsibility for our lives. Just as Jacob handed over the decision making to his mother, we hand over our decision making to our culture, the media, and our peers.

But there is also much we can learn from how Jacob grows later in his life. Years after the blessing incident, we find Jacob crossing a river. His family and possessions had been sent to the other side, and he was left all alone. For a man who disliked himself enough to manipulate others, even taking on the image of his brother, being alone must have been a frightening experience. When we are alone, we are on a battlefield where those unredeemed parts of ourselves open fire on us. The Bible tells us that while he was alone, Jacob wrestled with an unknown assailant. The mysterious stranger could not beat Jacob, so he touched his hip and dislocated it. The fight continued all night; Jacob refused to let the man go until he gave Jacob a blessing. The man demanded to know Jacob's name. Jacob told him, but his assailant gave him a new name.

New names were given in the Bible as a way of noting a radical and profound change in a person. The mystery fighter renamed Jacob "Israel." In Hebrew, *Jacob* means "trickster" and is linked to the concept of "crooked." *Israel* means "to struggle with God and humans" and also is linked to the idea of "straight." Harold Kushner wrote:

> At the end of the struggle, Jacob is injured and limping, but the Bible nonetheless describes him as shalem, a Hebrew word with connotations of wholeness, integrity, being at peace with oneself. The word is related to shalom, peace. . . . Shalom means wholeness, everything fitting together, nothing missing, nothing broken. Just as peace on the world scene means no fighting between nations, no quarrelling with other people, shalom for you as an individual means no fighting with yourself, no quarrelling between the two halves of your divided soul.[7]

Jacob tried to create a false self, a self that was not him. Through struggle and determination, through warfare with the

monsters that moved him away from his true self, he found shalom. And in this wholeness and balance, he found out his real
name, discovered his true self.

Ironically, by creating a false self, he showed us what he really
thought of his brother. He saw him simply as an obstacle, an object
blocking his path. When we project a false self and live by the rules
of an image-driven culture that turns humans into mere images,
we do the same to others. Jacob's victory over his sins allowed
him to see the image of God in his brother. Spiritual writers Carol
Ochs and Kerry Olitzky observe:

> Jacob did not pray to be healed—to be made whole—because
> he didn't know that he was wounded. It would be twenty years
> before he would wrestle with the angel at Jabbok. Some com-
> mentators suggest that he was really wrestling with his feelings
> towards his brother. That is why he was able to say, on seeing
> Esau, "Seeing you is like seeing the face of God." He could not
> see that face in Esau until he had confronted his sins.[8]

By mastering his own sins, not only did Jacob bring a sense
of shalom into his own life, but that shalom flowed into his other
relationships as well. Even when Jacob embraced a false self, even
when he chose to act instead of live, even when he preferred to
manipulate instead of embrace truth, God still saw someone created in his image. God looked beyond the mess and saw Jacob
redeemed.

A DIFFERENT KIND OF WINNING

Jacob used his personal power, control, and manipulation to try
to find his true self; yet he couldn't discover that true self until he
learned how to separate himself from all that externally defined

him, to give up control of his public image, to give over his life in a private struggle with himself and God, away from his wives, servants, sons, and possessions. Jacob gave everything he had in his battle to redeem himself. When he had no more strength, no reserves, when he had fought until he had nothing left—that's when he found his true self. One can imagine Jacob returning from his wrestle looking terrible on the outside. He would have been bruised and battered, probably wet and covered in mud, limping from a dislocated hip. Yet he was internally changed. He learned that he had to give up his hold on what defined him in this world to truly be blessed.

In his book *Storytelling: Imagination and Faith*, Christian storyteller and writer William J. Bausch tells the spiritual fable of the old man of Crete.⁹ The old man lived on the stunningly beautiful Greek island of Crete, and his love for his island was so great that when he knew the time of his death was coming, he asked his sons to carry him down to the beach so that he could die on his beloved island. As he breathed his last breath, he grasped a handful of the soil of Crete and died happy.

As the old man waited to enter heaven, God came out to meet him, telling him that the joy of heaven was his, and all he had to do was let go of the soil of Crete and then he could enter into eternal bliss. The old man couldn't face losing his island, so he stayed outside heaven with the soil still in his hand. God was determined to see the old man in heaven, so this time he went out to meet him in the form of one of his oldest friends. They chatted and shared a few drinks, like old times. God then told him that it was time to enter heaven, that all he had to do was let go of the soil of Crete. But he still couldn't do it, so he remained outside.

Much time passed by. The old man became older and weaker. This time God went to him in the form of his young granddaughter. They played together, and then the time came to enter heaven.

The old man had very little strength left and couldn't hold the soil in his hand, and the precious earth of his island slipped from his hand as his granddaughter led him through the pearly gates.

To his amazement, as he entered heaven, the first thing he saw was his beloved island of Crete.

This fable carries much spiritual wisdom. In order to hold on to his island, the old man first had to give it up. The same dynamic applies to our search for our true selves. To find our true selves, we first must give up our lives. We see this most clearly in the death and resurrection of Christ. The victory for humanity, the defeat of evil, death, sin, flesh, *sarx*, and injustice, comes through the giving up of life. This is the last but hardest part of our journey toward our true selves. It is the final step—to become our real selves, we must die to those parts of us that are not truly us. As Jesus said to his disciples, "Whoever wants to save their life will lose it, but whoever loses their life for me and for the gospel will save it" (Mark 8:35).

These words of Jesus remind us that we will never become the people we were meant to be in this life. We don't hold the white rocks with our true names this side of death. Until we pass into glory, our journey toward our true selves cannot be complete. We, with all believers, will wait for the final resurrection of the believers. It's important to understand this, for in the Bible, to know someone's name is to have power over that person. This is why God asked Adam to name the animals and why God wouldn't tell Moses his name was Yahweh when they met at the burning bush. We will know our names and have complete control over our true selves only when we are raised in glory with Christ in his new creation.

THE MONASTERY OF MARTYRS

I began this book by sharing an incident from the British reality show series *The Monastery*. So intrigued were people by the concept that the show had more than three million viewers. The monastery was inundated with calls from people wanting to schedule retreats. In response to the wave of interest, the abbot of the monastery, Christopher Jamison, decided to write a book for all the people who were interested in Christian spirituality but who had no background in faith. In the book Jamison tells the story of a small monastery of French monks in the countryside of Algeria. For approximately sixty years the monastery had been a Christian presence and a witness to the surrounding Muslim neighbors, with whom the monks enjoyed excellent relations. However, in the early 1990s, the monks found themselves caught up in a violent conflict between the Algerian government and radical Islamic rebels who wished to turn the country into an Islamic state, free of all foreigners. As most foreigners fled the country, the monks decided it was their duty to stay with their Muslim neighbors who were suffering at the hands of the rebels.

On Christmas Eve 1993, the monastery was taken over by an armed group of rebels. The monks knew that the rebels had recently massacred a group of Croatian Catholic construction workers. Courageously, the head of the monastery, aptly named Father Christian, demanded that the rebels leave so that he and his monks could celebrate the birth of Christ. The rebels left but promised they would be back. For two years, even as reports came in that other Christians had been killed by the rebels, the monks, against all odds, stayed, prayed, read the Bible, and served and witnessed to their Muslim neighbors. With the prospect of the rebels returning at any moment, the spiritual life of the monks took on a new intensity. They had found a new sense of life by living on the edge of death. By offering up their lives and living with the threat of death every day, they had discovered holiness.

Christopher Jamison wrote of the monks, "The origin of 'sacrifice' is the Latin *sacrum facere*—'to make holy.' So as you offer your life on the altar, God blesses you and makes you holy. During those two years the monks offered themselves in communion each day: in return, God blessed them and made them holy."[10] In early 1996 the rebels made good on their promise to return. Father Christian and six other monks were murdered, their throats sliced. They had found their true selves by giving up their lives.

THE IMAGE OF GOD BEHIND ALL
THE GOO AND MUCK

During the writing of this book, my first child, Grace, was born. When you find out that you are going to be a parent, others begin to share their birth experiences with you. Person after person told me that the birth of their child was the greatest moment in their life, that meeting their baby for the first time in the delivery room was the most meaningful and life-changing experience a person could have. I even heard of some research that showed that many people either reengaged with faith or came to faith for the first time after the birth of their first child, so significant was the experience. I remember as my wife and I waited, as we passed by our baby's due date, I saw a new father share on television how tears ran down his cheeks as he held his child for the first time. To say that I went into the delivery experience with high expectations is an understatement.

Most labors are long experiences, so when the nurses told me to take a break and go get some coffee, I was happy to take their advice and get a caffeine hit for the long night ahead. Barely through my coffee, I was called by the midwife to the birth suite. To everyone's surprise, the medical staff included, our baby was almost here. I threw my coffee in the trash and rushed to the room. *Hang on*, I thought to myself, *I'm not ready*. I hadn't prepared myself for this earth-shattering, life-changing experience. Before I knew it, my wife had delivered our daughter; my child was here. The obstetrician, in one swift move, placed our child on my wife's chest. It was supposed to be the most amazing moment of my life, the moment when I finally met my flesh-and-blood offspring. Yet as I looked down, I didn't see a baby. I saw something that looked more like a creature covered in strawberry jelly, shivering.

This moment did not feel spiritual; it felt weird. But then everything changed. I looked at my wife, her face beaming as she looked down at our child. Her little head was buried in my wife's chest, so I reached down and lifted her head to see her face for the first time. Her eyes locked with mine, and then it happened: that indescribable identification of the image of God in her, that spark in this tiny human's eye of the person she would become. I could somehow feel the potential of this shaking, crying little human. This was not a shivering creature; this was my daughter, Grace. From that second forward I could never imagine life without her. In a flash we were bound together. I was profoundly changed, and I knew my job was to do everything in my power to aid her in becoming the person God wants her to be.

I think I now understand in some small way how God feels as he sees us. Probably we initially appear to him like a newborn baby—messy and covered in goo and muck. But he looks beyond all that. He lifts our faces; he looks deep into our eyes and sees the image of God, the potential for shalom. He sees us fully redeemed, exactly as he designed us when he knitted us in our mothers' wombs. This is why he calls out to you. He is beckoning you from the future to become your true self. He holds in his hand a white rock with your true name on it.

NOT THE END

It was never my intention to simply write a book about finding our true identity in God in order to make us all feel warm fuzzies.

When we embark on the journey to find our true selves, when we begin to move toward shalom and balance in our lives, we do so understanding that such a discovery carries a responsibility. When I was a teenager, my father told me a story that has burned itself into my mind. It is the story of a young Australian soldier in World War I. Every muscle in his body straining, his heart pumping to the point of bursting, he ran. He had found himself alone behind enemy lines, sprinting through mud and over trenches, enemy German troops breathing down his neck. As he vaulted a bomb crater, he looked down to ensure that he didn't fall. He saw a crumpled corpse. In the split second that he jumped over the body, he locked eyes with the corpse and realized that it was not a dead body but an injured comrade. In that moment, just as I had recognized that spark of humanity and that image of God in my daughter, he saw life in the eyes of an injured, scared young soldier lying helpless.

Before he hit the ground, he had already made the decision to risk his life. He could not continue running, having seen that spark in his comrade's eyes. He stopped. Putting his life at risk, he reached down into the mud, slung the injured body over his shoulder, and carried his fellow soldier to safety.

My father told me this story as an illustration of what it is to find faith: the gift of finding your true self comes with responsibility.

Before his death at the hands of the Algerian terrorists, Father Christian wrote a letter to be opened in case of his death. He wrote of his and his monks' readiness to die for the gospel and for the people among whom they lived. But most poignantly, so sure of his impending death, Father Christian wrote the following message to the radical Islamic terrorist he was sure would return to kill him:

> To you, my last-minute friend, who will not have known what you are doing: yes, I want this thank you and this adieu to be for

you, too, because in God's face I see you. May we meet again as thieves in Paradise, if it pleases God, the Father of us both.[11]

Father Christian's life will never be held up for imitation by the world's media machine in the way that the public selves of celebrities are. But the holiness of his life rings throughout eternity as clear as a bell. This holiness enabled him not only to find his true self, but to look into the eyes of the terrorist who would cut his throat and see not a murderer but the spark of the image of God and the potential of his killer's redeemed, true self.

Once you begin to shed your media masks and false public self, you begin to walk the path of holiness and shalom toward your true self. You will find that you begin to see sparks of eternity in your own life. You will see tiny signs each day of how you are becoming more like Christ. But you will also begin to see that spark, that potential, in others. You will often see it in people who cannot see it in themselves—perhaps in a family member or friend. But other times you will look down into the mud and muck of contemporary life, and behind the public selves, the media masks, the actors in your life movie, the people turned into products, you will look into the eyes of others and you will see that undeniable spark of the image of God. And you will find your fingers fumbling in your pockets to find a white stone. Everything within you will wish that you could pass them that smooth, cold, tangible reminder that Jesus stands holding a white stone with their true name written on it.

And so I wish that I could reach into my pocket and hand you a white stone. But I cannot, so this book is my white stone to you. A stone that also works as a key, opening a doorway out of the cramped, stale confines of the horizontal self, filling you with the gusts of fresh air perfumed with the scent of eternity.

I Want to Recruit You!

This may be the end of this book, but it is really the beginning of a much more exciting journey. For I must be honest: I come with an agenda.

I want to recruit you.

I want to recruit you to become part of a revolution of the vertical self. More than ever individuals need to see themselves as God sees them. So many of the problems in our culture stem from a misunderstanding of our true identities.

Sadly, it is not only individuals who have come under the spell of the horizontal self; in the last twenty years, churches and ministries have, with good intentions, become sharper, hipper, and more relevant. Yet often these external changes have been matched by deterioration in the quality of the internal lives of the people filling them. The relevance of our churches' public image is negated by the irrelevance of our personal lives to a culture of people desperate to discover who they really are.

Things must change! This problem is not going to be solved

169

by T-shirts, plastic wrist bands, super-pastors, and slick programs. It will be solved by ordinary people like you and me embodying this new way of seeing our identities and encouraging others to do the same. So it is my goal to transform you from a passive reader into an active advocate and teacher of the vertical self. I need you to educate others about our need to change how we see ourselves, to become people defined by a vertical sense of self. So I would like to offer you the chance to be part of a "pass it on" movement. How do we do this? Read on.

BECOME A TEACHER OF THE VERTICAL SELF

Let's not beat around the bush; if you are to shake off the effects of living under the horizontal self, and if you are to journey toward your true self, you will need people to keep you accountable. You need some people who are going to be to you the Soul Friends described in chapter 10. So spend some time in prayer and ask God to reveal to you three people (I think three works best, but it could be fewer or more) who could keep you accountable as you journey toward your true self and who also need to be freed from the horizontal self—and who need to discover that Jesus stands in eternity with a white stone for them with their true name written on it. When you have your three names, write them down here.

Name_____

Name_____

Name_____

PASS IT ON!

Now, here is where the magic lies. Just imagine if the three people that you choose go on to each choose another three people and those people all do the same, and so on. You have the power of multiplication at work, and before you know it you have affected hundreds of people. Keep multiplying and you are talking about a movement of people discovering their true identities in Christ.

So how do you teach the other people about the vertical self? It's not that hard, really. Buy them a coffee or invite them over for a meal. You might use a napkin to sketch out the diagrams of the vertical and horizontal selves. You might just blurt out everything you learned in one long rant. You might buy them this book. You might rent *Breakfast at Tiffany's* and watch it together. You might work through the study guide at the back of this book with the three people that you have chosen. Your options are only limited by your imagination. So it does not matter how you do it; what matters is that you do it.

Let the movement toward our true selves begin!

Study Guide

f you've chosen to take the ideas in this book to the next level, this guide will help you in your journey. Here's what I recommend you gather before you begin:

1. **Some friends.** I reckon reading groups work best with numbers between five and twelve. But hey, that is just me.
   1a. **A notebook.** You'll need some writing space to jot down your thoughts or to use if you prefer to journal and work through these questions and exercises on your own, without a group.
2. **A place to meet.** Make sure that it is comfy, conducive to conversation, and convenient. Because this book is all about our culture, particularly the way we act in public, I strongly recommend that you meet in a public place, such as a café. Given the fact that this book deals with how we act in public, you will notice, often before your eyes, people living out the concept of the horizontal self. You will find that meeting in public also changes the

way we act and exposes the way in which we have been influenced by the horizontal self. This means that your interactions with this study guide will tend to be a lot more honest.

3. **Some books.** Get each member to grab a copy of this book and underline one key passage that grabs his or her attention each week.

4. **A commitment,** as a group, to treat this study seriously—to be honest, real, and supportive with each other as you encourage each other, as you move toward your true selves.

CHAPTER 1

Underline Time: (5 min.) Have one person read out loud the part of this week's reading they underlined and share with the group why it resonated with them.

Exercise: (15 min.) Take a trip to your local mall. If you can't do this, purchase a couple of magazines or catalogs and note the different constructed "personalities" and "identities" portrayed in the advertisements that you see. List in your notebook.

Discussion Questions:

Q) Try to describe, in short paragraphs, "Cool," "Sexy," and "Glamorous." Did you find this exercise easy or difficult? Why?

Q) What constructed personalities or identities have you seen people around you display or attempt to live out? Is there a constructed personality or identity you have attempted to live out? If so, what was it?

Q) This chapter notes that "we have unprecedented personal freedom, but our freedom is accompanied by a haunting sense of being lost." Do you or have you ever felt that sense of being lost? If so, describe what that experience is or was like.

Q) Read Romans 1:18–25. In what ways does this passage relate to what you have read in this week's chapter?

CHAPTER 2

Underline Time: (5 min.) Have one person read out loud the part of this week's reading they underlined and share with the group why it resonated with them.

Exercise: (15 min.) Make a list of everything you have spent money on in the last two weeks. How did the concept of the horizontal self affect your purchases or your shopping experience?

Discussion Questions:

Q) In what ways can you see our culture being influenced by the remnants of the idea of the vertical self? In what ways can you observe our culture being influenced by the idea of the horizontal self?

Q) Who is someone you know who displays the attributes of the vertical self most clearly? Can you think of someone who is caught up in the horizontal self? How did these different focuses affect his or her behavior?

Q) This chapter notes that people who live with a horizontal sense of self live under the judgment of their peers. Can you think of a time when you placed yourself under the judgment of your peers? How did this affect you?

Q) Read Genesis 1:26–30 and then Genesis 3:1–13. It could be said that the first passage from Genesis 1 represents humans living under a vertical sense of self, whereas the second reading, from Genesis 3 represents a move to a horizontal sense of self. Do you agree or disagree? Why?

CHAPTER 3

Underline Time: (5 min.) Have one person read out loud the part of this week's reading they underlined and share with the group why it resonated with them.

Exercise: (15 min.) Try and think of at least five movies in which the plot was about the main characters "finding themselves." What kind of activities and experiences did the protagonists engage in to "find themselves"?

Discussion Questions:

Q) Have you ever discovered yourself being a different person in different situations? How and why? Has this ever meant that you have acted in ways that are contrary to your values?

Q) Can you think of someone who has reconstructed his or her identity? Describe how this person changed. Have you ever changed or reconstructed your identity? Explain why you felt you needed to do this.

Q) This chapter speaks about our culture pushing us to project a "successful image" to our peers. Can you think of a time when you have projected a successful image to your friends?

Q) Read Deuteronomy 5:7–8. What relevance do these first two of the Ten Commandments have to the idea of constructing an identity?

Moment of Truth: Now that you as a group understand the concepts of the vertical and horizontal selves, you can begin the weekly practice of breaking into pairs in order to ask each other the Moment of Truth question: *"In the past week, when did you act out of a vertical sense of self, and when did you act out of a horizon-*

tal sense of self?" The purpose of this question is to really get our teeth into the way the horizontal sense of self has influenced our identities and assist us as we move toward living out of our true identity: people created in God's image. I would recommend that you pick the same partner each week, if possible, and that you pick someone of the same gender as you. You might want to end your time of sharing by praying with your partner.

CHAPTER 4

Underline Time: (5 min.) Have one person read out loud the part of this week's reading they underlined and share with the group why it resonated with them.

Exercise: (15 min.) Name the people you think are the three biggest celebrities in the world today. As a group, discuss how the public images of these celebrities have been crafted and manufactured. Ask what you really know about the actual reality of these people's lives versus their public personas.

Discussion Questions:

Q) How is celebrity culture affecting the everyday lives of people in our society?

Q) This chapter discusses the way movies operate almost as a kind of modern-day scripture. Is there a film that has influenced the way you live your life? How has it influenced you?

Q) This chapter makes the point that one of the consequences of the horizontal self is that often we find ourselves "acting" in front of our peers or acquaintances. Can you think of a time when you have done this? What influenced you to do this?

Q) This chapter ends by noting the ways in which Christian

faith is affected by the horizontal self, and it contains a list of the ways in which the horizontal self changes some key components of faith (see page 52). As a group, read through the list and discuss the ways you have seen these changes in action.

Moment of Truth: Break off into pairs in order to ask each other the Moment of Truth question: *"In the past week, when did you act out of a vertical sense of self, and when did you act out of a horizontal sense of self?"*

CHAPTER 5

Underline Time: (5 min.) Have one person read out loud the part of this week's reading they underlined and share with the group why it resonated with them.

Exercise: (15 min.) This chapter discusses the ways in which our culture has forgotten many of the Christian roots upon which it was built. As a group, try and think of some of the positive fruits of our culture that have been born out of the biblical imagination.

Discussion Questions:

Q) This chapter makes the point that when people don't know how to behave, they refer to the storehouse of "media memories" that movies and television have given them in order to know how to act. What are some examples of this phenomenon that you have observed?

Q) Have you ever met someone who seems to have an almost indefinable quality about them that draws people to them? If so, who? What was it about them that caused this reaction?

Q) This chapter notes that many of the disposable identities that our media culture gives us, such as the "Sexy," "Glam," and "Cool" identities, take us away from our true selves, yet they also contain echoes of our true selves. Do you agree or disagree? Why?

Moment of Truth: Break off into pairs in order to ask each other the Moment of Truth question: *"In the past week, when did you act out of a vertical sense of self, and when did you act out of a horizontal sense of self?"*

CHAPTER 6

Underline Time: (5 min.) Have one person read out loud the part of this week's reading they underlined and share with the group why it resonated with them.

Exercise: (15 min.) As a group, make a list of ways you have heard the adjective *sexy* used in the last week. What products, people, experiences, places, and objects was the word attached to? Who can name the most ridiculous example?

Discussion Questions:

Q) How does the concept of the "sexy self" affect our culture today? What pressures does it place on people in their everyday lives?

Q) This chapter discusses the way the disposable identity of the sexy self is almost disconnected from sex and is more about social power. Where have you seen this phenomenon at play?

Q) What struck you about the story of Marilyn Monroe? What are the lessons from this story for you personally?

Moment of Truth: Break off into pairs in order to ask each other the Moment of Truth question *"In the past week, when did you act out of a vertical sense of self, and when did you act out of a horizontal sense of self?"*

CHAPTER 7

Underline Time: (5 min.) Have one person read out loud the part of this week's reading they underlined and share with the group why it resonated with them.

Exercise: (15 min.) As individuals, without telling the rest of the group, write down the name of a person you think is the coolest person alive today. Then go around and share your answer with the group, and give reasons why the person you chose is cool.

Discussion Questions:

Q) What is defined as cool among your friends and peers? What is not cool?

Q) How have you personally been affected by the cult of cool? How has it affected your public self and purchasing choices?

Q) What is the punishment in our culture for not being cool?

Q) This chapter notes that behind the concept of cool is a deep desire for personal authenticity. Do you agree or disagree? If so why?

Moment of Truth: Break off into pairs in order to ask each other the Moment of Truth question: *"In the past week, when did you act out of a vertical sense of self, and when did you act out of a horizontal sense of self?"*

CHAPTER 8

Underline Time: (5 min.) Have one person read out loud the part of this week's reading they underlined and share with the group why it resonated with them.

Exercise: (15 min.) As a group, discuss the most glamorous place you have ever been. What made it glamorous?

Discussion Questions:

Q) This chapter makes the point that glamour in our culture is an attempt to grasp at mystery and transcendence. Do you agree? If so, can you think of any examples?

Q) Do you agree with the statement "Idolatry is misguided worship, yet it is still facilitated by a desire to worship"? Why or why not?

Q) Where have you seen the paradox of cool/ sexy/ glam at work?

Moment of Truth: Break off into pairs in order to ask each other the Moment of Truth question: *"In the past week, when did you act out of a vertical sense of self, and when did you act out of a horizontal sense of self?"*

CHAPTER 9

Underline Time: (5 min.) Have one person read out loud the part of this week's reading they underlined and share with the group why it resonated with them.

Exercise: (15 min.) As a group, read 1 Corinthians 15:40–44. Spend some time discussing what you imagine our future resurrection bodies will be like.

Discussion Questions:

Q) This chapter reminds us that in the future you will exist minus all of your current flaws, your fears, your dysfunctions, your jealousy, and your anger. This redeemed you is yourself, but with your positives amplified, your talents expanded, your attributes multiplied, and your maturity fulfilled. It is you exactly as God wished you to be. Share with the group how specifically your future self will be different from how you are now.

Q) This chapter tells the story of Dr. Kemp. Can you think of someone that you have met who is like Dr. Kemp? What made that person seem holy?

Q) Read 2 Timothy 1:8–9. Discuss these verses in light of the chapter you have read this week.

Moment of Truth: Break off into pairs in order to ask each other the Moment of Truth question, *"In the past week, when did you act out of a vertical sense of self and when did you act out of a horizontal sense of self?"*

CHAPTER 10

Underline Time: (5 min.) Have one person read out loud the part of this week's reading they underlined and share with the group why it resonated with them.

Exercise: (15 min.) People today desperately need to understand that they are created in the image of God and that they do not have to live with a horizontal self. As a group, discuss some ways you can communicate this vital message with others.

Discussion Questions:

Q) Read Colossians 1:15–17. This passage speaks of Christ being the first image, the image in which we find all of our identity. What would it look like for you to build your identity on Christ?

Q) This chapter talks about the daily assaults our God-given identities face. What specific ways do you personally experience this phenomenon?

Q) Discuss the concept of the *Yetzer Ha'ra*. How have you seen it at work in your own life?

Moment of Truth: Break off into pairs in order to ask each other the Moment of Truth question: "In the past week, when did you act out of a vertical sense of self, and when did you act out of a horizontal sense of self?"

CHAPTER 11

Underline Time: (5 min.) Have one person read out loud the part of this week's reading they underlined and share with the group why it resonated with them.

Exercise: (15 min.) As a group, brainstorm some ways you can keep each other accountable to live with a vertical concept of self after this study ends.

Discussion Questions:

Q) What would it look like to bring your desires under the lordship of Christ?

Q) This chapter discusses the story of Jacob. What similarities are there between your own life and the life of Jacob?

Q) Discuss the concept of giving up your sense of self to receive a sense of self.

Q) How can you live in a way that sees not only the image of God in yourself but in those you encounter?

Moment of Truth: Break off into pairs in order to ask each other the Moment of Truth question: *"In the past week, when did you act out of a vertical sense of self, and when did you act out of a horizontal sense of self?"*

Notes

Foreword

1. Peter Burke, *Popular Culture in Early Modern Europe* (New York: New York University Press, 1978), 185, 207.
2. Meredith B. McGuire, "Why Bodies Matter: A Sociological Reflection on Spirituality and Materiality," *Spiritus* 3 (Spring 2003): 1–18, 6. For the Duffy Quote, see Eamon Duffy, *The Stripping of the Altars: Traditional Religion in England c.1400-c.1580* (New Haven, CT: Yale University Press, 1992), 47.
3. G. K. Chesterton, *Orthodoxy* (New York: John Lane, 1909), 170.
4. G. K. Chesterton, *The Paradoxes of Mr. Pond* (New York: Dodd, Mead, 1944), 63.
5. I have discussed this in a number of my books. See, for example, the power of the both/and in my *SoulTsunami: Sink or Swim in New Millennium Culture* (Grand Rapids, MI: Zondervan Publishing House, 1999), 158–80, 370–71; and the chapter entitled "From Sharp to Fuzzy," in my *Carpe Mañana: Is Your Church Ready to Seize Tomorrow?* (Grand Rapids, MI: Zondervan, 2001), 125-39; the paradoxes of risk-taking in the chapter entitled "Walking the Gangplank: Risk Taking," in my *AquaChurch 2.0: Piloting Your Church in Today's Fluid Culture* (Colorado Springs, CO: WaterBrook, 2004, 55–61; the bell curve/well curve distinctions in my *The Gospel According to Starbucks: Living with a Grande Passion* (Colorado Springs: WaterBrook Press, 2007), 39–43. For my 1995 "double ring" video, where I argued that Jesus always appears to us in surround sound, see my Web site, www.leonardsweet.com.

Chapter 2

1. Patrick Dillon, *The Last Revolution: 1688 and the Creation of the Modern World* (London: Jonathan Cape, 2006).
2. A. N. Wilson, *The Victorians* (London: Arrow, 2002), 103–4.

Chapter 3

1. Kenneth J. Gergen, *The Saturated Self: Dilemmas of Identity in Contemporary Life* (New York: Basic, 1991), 73.
2. J. Richard Middleton and Brian J. Walsh, *Truth Is Stranger Than It Used to Be: Biblical Faith in a Postmodern Age* (Downers Grove, IL: InterVarsity, 1995), 56.
3. It is interesting to note that in the age of the horizontal self, our cultural language regarding sexuality speaks of *performance* and *achievement*, of mechanics rather than relationship.
4. Both of these presidential publicity stunts were highly planned and orchestrated events that deliberately played into the myths of popular culture to win political points. Such stunts are now employed by both sides of politics. The exploitation of the mythology of entertainment is bipartisan.
5. Jean M. Twenge, *Generation Me: Why Today's Young Americans Are More Confident, Assertive, Entitled—and More Miserable Than Ever Before* (New York: Free Press, 2006), 66–68.
6. Christopher Lasch, *The Culture of Narcissism: American Life in an Age of Diminishing Expectations* (New York: Warner, 1980).
7. Twenge, *Generation Me*, 68.

Chapter 4

1. Neal Gabler, *Life: The Movie: How Entertainment Conquered Reality* (New York: Knopf, 1998).
2. Ibid., 192.
3. Ibid., 197.
4. Thomas de Zengotita, *Mediated: How the Media Shapes Your World and the Way You Live in It* (London: Bloomsbury, 2005), 5.
5. Chris Rojek, *Celebrity* (London: Reaktion, 2001).
6. Days after I wrote this paragraph, a seemingly normal young man walked into a mall and shot several people dead. He left a note saying that his motivation was to become famous; he was prepared to pay the price of death and infamy to achieve his goal.
7. Rojek, *Celebrity*, 14.
8. Ibid., 15.
9. Ibid., 11.
10. Douglas Rushkoff et al., *The Merchants of Cool*, film, directed by Barak Goodman (New York: PBS, 2005), film.
11. A. N. Wilson, *The Victorians* (London: Arrow, 2002), 18–21.

Chapter 6

1. Ariel Levy, *Female Chauvinist Pigs: Women and the Rise of Raunch Culture* (New York: Simon & Schuster, 2006), 31.
2. Sean French, *Bardot* (London: Pavilion, 1994), 15.
3. Barbara Leaming, *Marilyn Monroe* (London: Weidenfeld & Nicholson, 1998), 426.

Chapter 7

1. Dick Pountain and David Robins, *Cool Rules: Anatomy of an Attitude* (London: Reaktion, 2000), 13.
2. Ibid., 19–20.
3. Ibid., 36.
4. Ibid., 38.
5. Daniel Harris, *Cute, Quaint, Hungry and Romantic: The Aesthetics of Consumerism* (New York: Da Capo, 2001), 52–53.
6. Thomas Frank, *The Conquest of Cool: Business Culture, Counterculture, and the Rise of Hip Consumerism* (Chicago: University of Chicago Press, 1997), 12.
7. Jack Kerouac, *Desolation Angels* (London: Flamingo, 1965), 351.
8. John Leland, *Hip: The History* (New York: HarperCollins, 2004), 8.

Chapter 8

1. *Breakfast at Tiffany's* is based on the short novel by Truman Capote of the same name. Fascinatingly, the character Holly Golightly was based on his mother, who attempted to escape her past of poverty in the South by re-creating herself as a sophisticated New York party girl.

Chapter 9

1. Robert N. Bellah et. al, *Habits of the Heart: Individualism and Commitment in American Life* (Los Angeles: University of California Press, 1985), 83.
2. Eugene Peterson, *Christ Plays in Ten Thousand Places: A Conversation in Spiritual Theology* (London: Hodder & Stoughton, 2005), 37–38.
3. Gordon Moyes, *When Box Hill Was a Village* (Homebush West, NSW: Anzea, 1991).
4. Ibid., 106–7.
5. Joseph Heath and Andrew Potter, *Nation of Rebels: Why Counterculture Became Consumer Culture* (New York: HarperCollins, 2005), 64.
6. Ibid, 62.
7. Jess Worth, "Buy Now, Pay Later," *The New Internationalist*, November 2006, 3.
8. Dallas Willard, *The Divine Conspiracy: Rediscovering Our Hidden Life in God* (London: Fount, 1998), 44.
9. Ibid.

Chapter 10

1. Richard Middleton, *The Liberating Image: The Imago Dei in Genesis 1* (Grand Rapids: Brazos, 2005).
2. Brian J. Walsh and Sylvia C. Keesmaat, *Colossians Remixed: Subverting the Empire* (Downers Grove, IL: InterVarsity, 2004), 63.
3. C. S. Lewis, *Mere Christianity* (San Francisco: Harper Collins, 2001), 203.
4. Anthony A. Hoekema, "The Reformed Perspective," in *Five Views on Sanctification*, ed. Stanley N. Gundry (Grand Rapids: Zondervan, 1987), 61–62.
5. Richard Foster, *Streams of Living Water: Celebrating the Great Traditions of Christian Faith* (London: HarperCollins, 1998), 82.
6. Walter Hilton, "The Ladder of Perfection," in *The English Mystics of the Fourteenth Century*, ed. Karen Armstrong (London: Kyle Cathie, 1991), 137.
7. N. T. Wright, *Paul: In Fresh Perspective* (London: Society of Promoting Christian Knowledge, 2005), 35.
8. Ibid.
9. Ibid.
10. *The Simpsons.* Season 5, episode no. 7, "Bart's Inner Child," first broadcast 11 November 1993 by Fox Network. Directed by Bob Anderson and written by Matt Groening and George Meyer.
11. St. Augustine of Hippo, *Confessions*, trans. R. S. Pine-Coffin (London: Penguin, 1961), 164.
12. Harold Kushner, *Living a Life That Matters: Resolving the Conflict Between Conscience and Success* (New York: Knopf, 2001), 15.
13. George Robinson, *Essential Judaism: A Complete Guide to Beliefs, Customs and Rituals* (New York: Pocket Books, 2000), 245.
14. Alan Morinis, *Everyday Holiness: The Jewish Spiritual Path of Mussar* (Boston: Trumpeter, 2007), 25.
15. P. J. O'Rourke, *All the Trouble in the World: The Lighter Side of Famine, Pestilence, Destruction and Death* (Sydney: Picador, 1994), 9.
16. M. Scott Peck, *The Road Less Traveled: A New Psychology of Love, Traditional Values and Spiritual Growth* (New York: Simon & Schuster, 1988), 298.
17. 1 Timothy 3:1–13.
18. Morinis, *Everyday Holiness*, 26.
19. The gospel of John, like the whole New Testament, was written in Greek, the *Lingua Franca* of the day. So the Greek word *eirene* is used for peace instead of the Hebrew *shalom*. For the Greek-speaking communities of the Jewish diaspora, *eirene* still would have carried the breadth of meaning that *shalom* carried in the Old Testament.
20. Jacques Ellul, *The Meaning of the City* (Grand Rapids: Eerdmans, 1970), 1, 3.
21. Quoted in Ray Simpson, *Exploring Celtic Spirituality: Historic Roots for Our Future* (London: Hodder & Stoughton, 1995), 114.

22. Protestants, with their Reformation heritage, have often balked at such suggestions of restitution because they seem like attempts to find salvation through works. Although that strain definitely exists within some forms of Christianity, what we are talking about here is not an attempt to be justified before God but rather ridding ourselves of the polluting effects of sin on our well-being—an exercise in spiritual discipline, not salvation by works.

23. Simpson, *Exploring Celtic Spirituality*, 114.

24. Morinis, *Everyday Holiness*, 53.

25. C. S. Lewis, "The Weight of Glory," in *Screwtape Proposes a Toast and Other Pieces* by C. S. Lewis (London: Fontana, 1965), 94–95.

26. Philip Yancey, *Rumors of Another World: What on Earth Are We Missing?* (Grand Rapids: Zondervan, 2003), 35, 37.

27. Donald Ritchie, *The Image Factory: Fads and Fashions in Japan* (London: Reaktion, 2003), 28–29.

Chapter 11

1. Shmuley Boteach, *Kosher Adultery: Create Erotic Desire: Seduce and Sin with Your Spouse* (Avon, MA: Adams Media, 2002), 8–9.

2. "The Life of Pelegia the Harlot," in *The Desert Fathers*, trans. Helen Waddell (New York: Vintage, 1998), 186–87.

3. Ibid.

4. *The Life of St. Teresa of Avila by Herself*, trans. J. M. Cohen (London: Penguin, 1957), 13.

5. Quote taken from Rodney Clapp's fantastic essay "That Glorious Mongrel: How Jazz Can Correct the Heresy of White Christianity," in Rodney Clapp, *Border Crossing: Christian Trespasses on Popular Culture and Public Affairs* (Grand Rapids: Brazos, 2000), 195.

6. Kushner, *Living a Life That Matters*, 22.

7. Ibid., 28–29, 89.

8. Carol Ochs and Kerry M. Olitzky, *Jewish Spiritual Guidance: Finding Our Way to God* (San Francisco: Jossey-Bass, 1997), 145.

9. William J. Bausch, *Storytelling: Imagination and Faith* (Mystic, CT: Twenty-Third Publications, 1984), 127–28.

10. Abbot Christopher Jamison, *Finding Sanctuary: Monastic Steps for Everyday Life* (London: Orion, 2006), 163.

11. Ibid., 162.

Interview with
the Author

TN: Do you ever find yourself living out of a horizontal sense of self, or have you reached a monklike level of immunity?

MS: I find myself falling for it all the time. I think our culture is so drenched in the worldview of the horizontal self that it is almost impossible not to be affected in some way. What I have found, though, is the more I really put into practice what I was writing about, that slowly, bit by bit, I worry a lot less about what my peers and the public think about me. The only way to get to that point is with God's help and with discipline and people helping me along the way. I have found, also, that a great way to rid yourself of the horizontal self is to not take yourself too seriously and always to be ready to make a joke at your own expense. If you can't mock yourself in front of others, you probably are still well entrenched.

TN: So, then, are you proposing that Christians should avoid fashion or any sense of trying to make a statement with how we style ourselves?

MS: Not at all. Often people hear me teach about the vertical self and assume that I am expecting them to go and wear a hessian sack. This could not be further from what I mean. God is the Creator and created us as creative beings; every culture throughout history has used styling and fashion to express that creativity. The answer is not to reject fashion and aesthetics but rather to place them under the lordship of Christ. Fashion, placed in its correct place in God's order, can be an act of worship.

TN: So you're saying that Christians shouldn't avoid being cool altogether?

MS: This is a funny one. What I learned while researching the book is that seemingly the more you try to be cool, the less cool you are. But then the less you worry about being cool and what anyone thinks of you, often people will strangely start to see you as cool. This is what I call the paradox of cool. The more whole we become, the more we root our identities in Christ, the more people will be drawn to us.

Having said that, there is almost a mythic belief in some Christian circles that the answer to the church's marginal position in the West is simply to become cool. I have a real issue with this. Yes, there is a need for us to be relevant and culturally conversant. But come on! Do we really believe that there are millions of people out there who will become Christians when we as believers reach the required level of hipness? There was a survey done, I think it was done here in Australia, that asked people outside the church if they would consider attending if Church became contemporary culturally. Only a minimal amount said yes.

I often ask groups when I teach if they thought the movie *Napoleon Dynamite* was cool. Most put their hands up. I then tell the group that the movie was made by Mormons. I then ask them how many of them would consider becoming part of the Church of Latter Day Saints now that they know that a movie that they thought was cool was made by Mormons. No one has ever put their hand up.

TN: **You live in Australia, whereas the majority of your readers are here in the United States. Does the horizontal self play out differently in the two cultures; and if so, how?**

MS: In our age of globalization, you can encounter the horizontal self all over the place. I saw a documentary about "Sexting" (sending sexual text messages) in Saudi Arabia. In the documentary young women fully covered in veils were sending these suggestive messages to young guys, and vice versa, via Bluetooth. It was amazing how, underneath this conservative Islamic culture, the message of the horizontal self was living out. So you can find this phenomenon all over the globe.

Australians tend to be a bit less extroverted than Americans, so often our horizontal selves are more subtle, but it is still just as prevalent. I also find that it depends where you are and what the culture of your city is. For example, Miami and Sydney would have a much more beach-orientated, "body image-" driven expression of the horizontal self. Whereas my home town of Melbourne would be more like a Seattle or Portland in terms of its colder weather and artiness, and it would have a horizontal self based on wearing black, coffee culture, and convincing the world how hip and cosmopolitan we are.

TN: **You write briefly that in the age of the horizontal self, Christian leaders are transformed into celebrities. Can you elaborate?**

MS: Our culture across the board has been affected by celebrity culture and what I would label the rise of the celebrity self. It used to be that celebrity was confined to the entertainment industry, sports, politics, and the arts. But now celebrity affects every industry and niche. We have superstar cooks and gardeners, financial advisors and computer gamers. So it is no wonder that Christian culture is shaped by this trend. Also, technology is making it more possible for Christian leaders to appear like celebrities. Things like Twitter create a false intimacy. A Christian leader may tweet that he just had an espresso with his wife whilst on vacation—seemingly harmless thing to do, but it will lead thousands of their followers to feel that they have an intimate connection with that leader when in fact they don't. This is the essence of porn, which is an illusion of intimacy devoid of relationship. In porn, the viewer turns the subject into an object to be consumed. In our world of overfamiliarity, leaders can easily turn themselves into images and thus fuel both the worship (note the word) of celebrity and the horizontal self.

We live in a culture of false intimacy and familiarity. Johnny Carson was often criticized by people who met him for being aloof and distant. Carson's friend and fellow comedian Steve Martin countered that Carson was not distant—he simply did not assume that intimacy was there when it was not; he preferred politeness to faux familiarity. It preserved the dignity of both Carson and the people whom he encountered. I think Christian leaders can learn a lot from this. We need to remember that the age we live in means that we can communicate with ease, but let's remember that we are communicating the gospel, not ourselves. Just look at Jesus. He was God in human form, and yet he always points the glory back to his father. He was the Messiah but was constantly running away from crowds and their messianic expectations of him because he understood his mission. Leaders can learn a lot from his examples. Jesus is the most known person in history, yet he was an anti-celebrity in that he subverts all of our expectations of the famous.

TN: You tend to refer to older stars and celebrities in this book; why not newer celebrities?

MS: Two reasons: firstly, things are moving so fast now that it almost seems that bands and celebrities have a much shorter life span. Name a band or an "it" girl and you can be sure that by the time your book comes out, the star will be out of the spotlight. Secondly, pretty much any band or star today borrows from the older stars so much that I thought I would go back to the sources. Look at any indie band today and you will see elements of Bob Dylan, the Velvet Underground, and the Stones. The latest sex symbol being touted by men's magazines is just a replica of Bardot, Monroe, or early Fonda. The latest Hollywood hunk is almost always a photocopy of Brando or James Dean. The latest art sensation is going to be a mix of Jackson Pollock, Dali, or Warhol. There is very little new today.

TN: You must have read a lot of biographies of celebrities for this book; what was that like?

MS: I read stacks; a lot of celebs I researched did not get into final draft of the book. Even Prince and Michael Jackson got a read; I think my wife thought I was becoming obsessed for a while there. But I really wanted to get my head around this whole idea of the celebrity. One interesting thing was discovering how some stars came close to something like faith at the end of their lives. Beat writer Jack Kerouac, at the end of his life, despite living this hedonistic existence and flirting with Buddhism, started coming to the conclusion that the only true thing was the cross. He spent his last years painting all of these crosses. Andy Warhol, who perhaps more than anyone embodied or expressed the horizontal self, had this hidden vertical self in which he would take communion daily, go and pray with his elderly mother, and would, in disguise, go and work in soup kitchens. He also, like Kerouac, painted lots of images of Christ in his later years.

TN: Is the horizontal self primarily an issue facing just youth and young adults?

MS: No. The horizontal self affects all age groups. The post–World War II culture saw the creation of the first real youth generation—the baby boomers. So anyone under seventy who was raised in the West has grown up with that mentality. If you are twenty now, you are the grandchild of the youth generation. So the whole vertical self is deeply entrenched in almost all age groups of our culture.

TN: What do you do, then, if you know someone who is totally caught up in the horizontal self?

MS: Our culture promises us a cavalcade of delights, and although it does not deliver, the illusion is pretty strong. So it is hard to convince someone who is caught up in a horizontal self that they are heading down a bad path. Firstly, we must pray for them. Also it is really key that *you* are living out of a vertical self. I really do think that when we do this, people see something in us. So the key to helping someone is modeling better, alternative "ourselves."

About the Author

M ark Sayers is a writer, thinker and sought-after speaker who specializes in the relationship between faith and culture. He is the founder of Über, a ministry that focuses on issues of youth and young-adult culture and discipleship. He is also senior leader of Red Church in Melbourne, Australia, where he lives with his wife, Trudi, and daughter, Grace. Find out more about Mark's ministry and follow his blog at www.marksayersthinks.com.

What if you're living in the wrong *reality?*

Our shopping mall world offers us a never-ending array of pleasures to explore. Consumerism promises us a vision of heaven on earth—a reality that's hyper-real. We've all experienced hyperreality: a candy so "grape-ey" it doesn't taste like grapes any more; a model's photo so manipulated that it doesn't even look like her; a theme park version of life that tells us we can have something better than the real thing. But what if this reality is not all that it's cracked up to be? Admit it: we've been ripped off by our culture and its version of reality that leaves us lonely, bored, and trapped. But what's the alternative?

In *The Trouble With Paris*, pastor Mark Sayers shows us how the lifestyles of most young adults actually work against a life of meaning and happiness to sabotage their faith. Sayers shows how a fresh understanding of God's intention for our world is the true path to happiness, fulfillment, and meaning.

 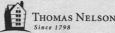